S0-ABD-125

VOLUNTEER ORIENTATION AND TRAINING

Marlene Wilson, General Editor

Group's Volunteer Leadership Series™
Volume 5
Group's Church Volunteer Central™

Loveland, Colorado

Group's Volunteer Leadership Series™, Volume 5

Volunteer Orientation and Training

Copyright © 2004 Group Publishing, Inc.

Visit our Web site: **www.grouppublishing.com**

Credits
Writer: Mikal Keefer
Editors: Mikal Keefer and Scott Kinner
General Editor: Marlene Wilson
Chief Creative Officer: Joani Schultz
Art Director: Nathan Hindman
Cover Designer: Jeff Storm
Production Manager: Peggy Naylor

Produced with the assistance of The Livingstone Corporation (www.LivingstoneCorp.com). Project staff includes Chris Hudson, Ashley Taylor, Mary Horner Collins, Joel Bartlett, Cheryl Dunlop, Mary Larsen, and Rosalie Krusemark.

Library of Congress Cataloging-in-Publication Data

Volunteer orientation and training / Marlene Wilson, general editor.—1st
        American hardbound ed.
      p. cm. — (Group's volunteer leadership series ; v. 5)
      ISBN 0-7644-2749-0 (alk. paper)
      1. Voluntarism—Religious aspects—Christianity. 2. Christian
leadership. 3. Church work. 4. Volunteers—Training of. I. Wilson, Marlene. II. Series.
BR115.V64V65 2003
253'.7–dc22   2003022122

10 9 8 7 6 5 4 3 2 1   12 11 10 09 08 07 06 05 04

Printed in the United States of America.

Contents

Contents

Introduction

Why being intentional about setting up an orientation program and training program makes sense for your ministry.

Remember how the first day on a new job feels?

You want to make a great impression, so you show up exactly on time—or early. You're nervous about the work, whether it'll be something you master quickly or something that leaves you baffled.

Will your job be as described during the interview, or are you walking into something bigger than you expected? Where will you sit? Will you be able to use the new computer programs? Have you dressed appropriately? Will you fit in? Are people friendly?

You have a hundred questions, but they all boil down to this: Will I be successful?

Starting a new job—as a paid employee or a volunteer—can be intimidating. There's so much information to learn . . . so many logistics to master . . . so many people to get to know. It's all a bit overwhelming.

And through it all there's a steady drumbeat of desire to do the job well—to be successful.

That means your volunteers want precisely what you want: for them to hit the ground running when they start their volunteer jobs, and to accomplish great things. You want for them to be successful.

You're well on your way to creating a successful volunteer ministry. You've drafted job descriptions, recruited great people, carefully interviewed, and placed people in volunteer jobs that fit like a glove.

Now it's time to take the next step by providing intentional, targeted orientation and training programs.

In a nutshell, an orientation program answers the question: What is it like to live or work here? A training program answers the next question that usually follows: What does it take to be successful here?

When a volunteer has the answers to both those questions, you dramatically increase that volunteer's comfort . . . effectiveness . . . and likelihood of sticking in the job.

You win. The volunteer wins. The ministry wins. The people your ministry serves win. And everyone gets to be successful.

Orientation Defined

Orientation is a process, not a one-shot program. Here's how to create a process that meets the needs of your volunteers— and your paid ministry staff, too.

For years you've entered your name in contests, filling out little cards and sending in box tops for drawings, and for years your name has never been drawn—until now.

The knock on your door was official notification that you're the Grand Prize Winner, and your all-expenses-paid trip to Italy will begin immediately. You've got just enough time to stuff two suitcases full of the clothes you think you'll need for your week in beautiful Tuscany, where you'll stay at a private villa.

Within an hour you're whisked away by limousine to the airport, where a chartered jet wings you away on your whirlwind journey.

On the way, you use the complimentary phone to call everyone you can think of: family, friends, even people you hardly know. A private secretary is at your house, cleaning, filling the dishwasher, and phoning the Curl Up & Dye Hair Salon to cancel your appointment since Giuliano (who coifs all the Italian movie stars) will visit the villa to give you a complete makeover.

The jet lands and you're given your choice of any rental car you want, including the sporty red convertible you've long wished you could afford back home. You hop in, a map spread out on the seat beside you, and with the radio blaring opera you're soon winding your way through the rolling hills of Tuscany, the landscape lush with vineyards, olive trees, and cypress groves.

Unfortunately, as you approach a medieval town carved into a hillside, you find the road growing narrow—too narrow for your car. Your villa, unfortunately, rests high above the town on a rocky outcrop. There's no way to reach the villa except through the town's center, where cobbled streets were designed for horses, not horsepower. You should have taken a scooter instead of a car.

> **"You're soon winding your way through the rolling hills of Tuscany."**

You schlep your suitcases up through town, smiling and nodding as you go. This is the Tuscany of your dreams, but it's also the Tuscany that's off the beaten tourist path. Few people can give you directions in English, so your search for the specific road that will take you to the villa is long, torturous, and extremely uphill.

You no sooner reach the villa (the view is *magnifico*, by the way) when you toss your laptop on the marble desktop. You dig the adaptor you bought when you were hoping to visit another country someday out of your computer case, plug it in, and immediately fry your computer. Nobody told you that household current is 220 volts in Italy, not the 110 your trusty laptop was wired to lovingly accept. You won't be e-mailing home to tell people about the wonderful time you're having.

Nor will you be doing much walking through the charming town, as you brought sandals and you're already feeling blisters form. You had no idea that the main form of transportation in this town was walking.

So sitting in Tuscany, in a villa that would be right at home in *Italian Dream Vacations* magazine, you stamp your foot (which pops a blister) and shout, "Why didn't someone tell me about this place?"

What you needed—and didn't get—was an orientation.

When you don't have enough information about an environment where you'll spend time—even wonderful Tuscany—the experience can be horrible. You're unprepared for the terrain. You don't know what to expect from the people you'll meet. You don't know the culture, how to accomplish things, or who to call for help. You feel alone and vulnerable.

And to a volunteer walking into a junior high boys Sunday school class for the first time, that's exactly how it feels.

You've invested a great deal of time and energy in finding, interviewing, and placing volunteers. If you fail to orient those volunteers into your ministry and their unique roles in it, you may well undo all you've accomplished.

There's tremendous power in a well-run orientation process. Not only can it salvage a Tuscan vacation, it can also keep your volunteers happy and on board.

The Power and Benefits of an Orientation Process

Notice that orientation is being referred to as a *process,* not just a *program.* That's because to be effective, an orientation will take more than a one-shot program—even if that program stretches over several days.

Remember: An orientation answers the question, "What's life like around here?" That's not a question that can usually be answered quickly, or in one session. It's something a new volunteer discovers over the course of time.

> "An orientation answers the question, 'What's life like around here?'"

You can help that discovery process along, and in this volume we'll tell you how. It's good to have a formal orientation program as a kickoff, but don't make the mistake of thinking that will be enough. It won't, at least for most volunteers.

The nuts and bolts of a volunteer's job are described on his or her job description . . . but job descriptions tell new volunteers what they'll be doing, not what life is like. Job descriptions leave lots of questions unanswered, such as . . .

- "Where's the closest bathroom?"

- "If I leave my lunch in the church refrigerator, will someone steal it?"

- "Is it okay to tell jokes and laugh around here?"

Deliver a great orientation for your volunteers and you'll answer their questions. You'll put them at ease. And . . .

You'll reassure volunteers they made a good decision by volunteering.

If the orientation is positive and helpful, it reinforces the volunteer's decision to be involved. It's not the first impression your volunteer ministry has made, but it's the first significant taste of the actual job. In a world where promises are often made ("you'll enjoy this volunteer role—sign up and find out for yourself!") and then broken, your follow-up will be noticeable and appreciated.

Scott, a volunteer in an Indiana church, describes his first volunteer role at the church he attended: "I was asked by a ministry leader to direct the Wednesday evening children's program for a period of three months. I checked to make sure my schedule was clear, then jumped on the opportunity.

"After I accepted, the ministry leader looked at me, patted me on the back, and said, 'I'm so sorry. Good luck.'

"That leader didn't reassure me at all. Basically he told me I'd made a mistake by taking the bait, that I'd soon regret it, and that heading up that program was the most difficult thing I'd ever do."

Fortunately, Scott immediately recruited a few close friends to help him with the program, and the three months were a blast for the leaders and the kids. But if Scott hadn't been the enthusiastic guy he is, he could easily have quit before he ever reached his first Wednesday night.

You'll connect the volunteer ministry to the larger purpose of the church.

Here's your chance to cement in a volunteer's mind how his or her job contributes to the larger mission of the church.

There are a dozen versions of a story that communicates this concept well. Here's one version you can share with your volunteers. Consider including it in your orientation programs to help volunteers catch a vision for how every job is important and contributes to the cause. One manager gives each new person on his team a copy of this story and a cobblestone to use as a paperweight.

During the middle ages, a Swiss bishop made the long journey to Germany to see the Frankfurt Cathedral. Still under construction after a hundred years, the cathedral would someday be the largest in Europe, a magnificent monument to God. A place where thousands would gather and worship.

The portly cleric rode through mountain passes into Germany. Miles from Frankfurt, the bishop could see the unfinished cathedral towering over the town, an enormous skeleton of supports and timbers. Massive gray walls rose where stone masons slowly fitted together row after row of huge blocks.

Eventually, the bishop stood in the very shadow of the cathedral. Around him swarmed an army of engineers, stonecutters, and carpenters. Crew chiefs shouted orders, pulleys creaked as stones were pushed and pulled into position, and the pounding of chisels and hammers echoed off soaring walls.

The bishop touched the arm of a man hurrying past. "Tell me what you're doing," the bishop said.

"I've got to recalculate the angle of the nave roof before we all get crushed," snapped the man. "Step aside!" And with that the man huffed away.

The bishop noticed a half-dozen laborers holding a rope that wound up into the distant darkness above, then back down where it was tied around a large stone block.

"What are you doing?" asked the bishop.

The workers exchanged annoyed glances. "Well, Father," said one, "we're hoisting this block up to the top—unless you can talk God into floating it there." The men laughed, squared their grip on the thick rope, then leaned into their back-breaking task.

The bishop saw a small, elderly man sitting near a doorway. He was hunched over, chiseling cobblestones. The bishop's heart went out to the man—obviously a stonemason whose age and failing eyesight made him good for nothing but this thankless task. A craftsman whose life had been reduced to chiseling stones for a walkway in some forgotten corner.

"And you," said the bishop. "Tell me what you're doing."

The old man looked up without missing a beat. "Me? I'm doing the same as everyone else—to God's glory, I'm building a cathedral."

A well-crafted orientation program helps volunteers see the importance of what they're doing. It's an opportunity for them to discover how their roles serve God, advance the work of the church, and have eternal significance.

You'll reduce volunteer turnover.

There's a direct correlation between orientation and retention. You've placed volunteers where their abilities, skills, and passions connect with a volunteer role, but they're not yet at home in that role. During their orientation you'll help them feel comfortable—and a volunteer who's comfortable, challenged, and growing is one who's likely to stick.

On the other hand, if a volunteer feels unwelcome—for any reason—that volunteer isn't likely to be with you long.

You'll help volunteers be successful in two ways—culture and information.

Matching a volunteer with the right job is only part of what sets a person up for success. The volunteer also has to match up with the culture where she's serving and master the information that's required for her to be successful.

Let's start by considering what happens when the culture of the volunteer collides with the culture of the ministry area . . .

Connecting with Culture: Jackie and the Whoopee Cushion

Jackie is a quiet, serious musician who wants to join her church's music ministry. She's sung in choirs since she was a girl, and she has a high regard for the dignity and majesty of choral music. Her choir experience has always been in choirs that prepared thoroughly and performed complicated choral pieces brilliantly.

She's gifted, skilled, and eager to sign on as a volunteer vocalist. To Jackie, serving in this spot seems like a match made in heaven. She can't wait for the first practice session.

Except the church's approach to music ministry is to lead worship, not to perform. And the music team isn't all that worried about hitting every note perfectly, or choosing challenging choral pieces. By intent the group selects easy-to-sing worship choruses and plays in an accessible, simple way so everyone can join in.

Plus, it's a tight-knit group that has fun as well as does ministry. During Jackie's first practice session the bass player leaves a whoopee cushion under the pad on the piano stool. The loud "pfffffffft" that echoes around the sanctuary when the keyboard player sits down prompts so much laughter that even the music director is howling hysterically.

What are the odds that Jackie will last as a member of the music ministry? that she'll even survive her first night of practice with the team?

In spite of her many musical gifts, there's a total disconnect when it comes to culture. In Jackie's case the distance might be so great that nothing could help her bridge the gap—but an orientation would be helpful. And it might be enough.

> "What are the odds that Jackie will last?"

At the very least, an orientation to the music ministry and its culture would keep Jackie from being scandalized and angry.

Granted, Jackie's case is extreme. But even for people who don't have to figure out how to transition from the Mormon

Tabernacle Choir to the Mostly Tentative Choir, culture can be a problem.

And it's a problem you can solve by taking volunteers through an orientation.

Orientation is where you cover culture—and help volunteers decide how they'll fit in. You'll give new volunteers the understanding and tools they need to effectively enter into new roles, surrounded by new people, working on new teams.

You can't overstate the impact of culture on a volunteer's experience. If volunteers don't understand how people communicate, or embrace the values of your ministry, they'll never feel at home.

> "Orientation is where you cover culture."

But how do you communicate culture? Let's answer that question by first examining what components combine to create our culture at church, and in our ministry.

Communication

There's probably a distinct approach to how you connect with other people in your church. Are titles important? Do you speak to each other directly, or is there a fair amount of caution in expressing opinions? Is there a "chain of command" to be respected, or can a volunteer speak to anyone about anything? How are messages and ideas shared?

Information

How is it distributed? Is it widely shared, or does confidentiality play a role that must be respected? How does a volunteer go about learning things?

Technology

How highly regarded is the latest technology? What does a volunteer need to know—and why?

Power

Who's in charge? What's their style of sharing—or not sharing—

power? How is power expressed? What are volunteers allowed to decide on their own? For what must they seek approval, and from whom?

Economics

How is money viewed in the ministry? What's scarce and must be used carefully, and what seems to be always available in abundance? How do people go about getting what they need?

Values

What does the ministry hold in high regard? What does it believe? How are those beliefs expressed? How thoroughly are the values integrated in the culture—is everyone on board? How clear are the preferred values?

Tradition

What traditions are part of how things are done? Who's the keeper of the flame for the traditions? Are the traditions embraced, tolerated, or somewhere in between? How are the traditions celebrated?

Rules and regulations

What are the rules that maintain order in the culture? How are those rules structured? What are the penalties for breaking the rules?

Tone

What's the emotional tone of the culture? Is it okay to have fun? How much fun? How do people have fun? Are there times the culture demands solemnity? When and why?

Change

How open is the culture to changing things? What sort of things are changeable, and which are "sacred cows" that seem immune to change? How does one go about instigating change?

Pecking order

Who's important and who's less important? How is that demonstrated? How are segments of people divided—and why?

Who is "the enemy"?

Is there a cause that the culture seeks to promote, or a group or cause that has been identified as the enemy? What cause will encourage the culture to circle the wagons or send out the sentries?

Watering holes

Where does the culture gather for support and sustenance? Where is the culture in evidence and celebrated?

> "Acclimating to a new culture is an ongoing process."

Acclimating to a new culture is an ongoing process. Allow time and opportunity for it to happen. It's simply not possible to work through a list of cultural elements like those listed above in one brief meeting.

And a word of caution: You might think that because someone was raised in your church and already knows the people with whom he or she will be serving, there's no need for an orientation. You would be wrong. There's a huge difference between being a student in a class and teaching the class. And what's valued in the high school youth group will vary dramatically from what's valued in the preschool ministry.

In addition to covering culture, orientations will help volunteers in another way . . .

Connecting with Information: Mrs. Brown and the Missing Envelopes

Orientation is also where you can shorten the learning curve for volunteers. You can tell them what they need to know instead of hoping they'll figure it out on their own . . . something that may never happen.

At one church, the Sunday school superintendent received

a complaint from the offering usher about Mrs. Brown, a Sunday school teacher who failed to turn in the offering collected in her second grade classroom. Other teachers placed the change they collected in envelopes, then slid the envelopes under their classroom doors. The designated offering usher went down the hallway collecting envelopes while classes were underway.

There was never an envelope outside Mrs. Brown's door.

Theories were floated. Was she pocketing the estimated two dollars in change each Sunday? spending it on classroom supplies? failing to take an offering at all? What could be done? What should be done? Did the pastor know?

Finally, the supervisor asked Mrs. Brown about the class offering. She replied that no one had ever told her about any envelope procedure. She'd been collecting the money in Sunday school, then dropping it in the offering plate an hour later when a collection was taken during church.

Mrs. Brown had circumvented the offering envelope procedure, but still accomplished the goal: Offering money was collected and turned in. Once the process was explained, without fail an envelope scooted out from under her door each Sunday. Satisfied, the offering usher declared Mrs. Brown a success.

What information you share in an orientation meeting depends on what you want to accomplish. Do you have a clear purpose and set of objectives? Without them, you don't have much chance of having a meaningful orientation meeting. Nor will you know if you were effective in meeting your objectives.

> "What information you share depends on what you want to accomplish."

Whatever you settle on as objectives for your orientation process, be sure you're hitting them by measuring results. It may be a year or more before you have enough volunteers entering or leaving the program to be able to determine impact, but it's important to begin now. The sooner you start, the sooner you'll know how to tweak volunteer orientations so you're making the most of the program.

- If your objective was to transmit information, administer a test to be sure volunteers are learning and retaining the information.

- If your objective was to reduce volunteer turnover, track whether volunteers exposed to the orientation program stayed longer than other volunteers.

- If your objective was to help volunteers become effective sooner, do interviews with volunteers six weeks into their volunteer experience. Ask how what they covered in orientation helped—or hindered—their ability to master their jobs.

Whatever your objectives, it's likely you'll be sharing information at orientation meetings. Since that's a given, be careful about selecting what information you'll include. Ask yourself and, perhaps, your task force:

> "As you answer these questions, three things will quickly become obvious."

- What information has proven to be most useful to new volunteers?

- Who is best suited to present the information?

- When is the information most appropriately presented?

- What logistical information do new volunteers need?

- What problems and challenges are typically encountered by new volunteers?

- What policies and procedures do new volunteers need to know?

As you answer these questions, three things will quickly become obvious . . .

Not every volunteer needs precisely the same information.
For instance, a Sunday morning greeter might need a far more detailed awareness of how the building is laid out than the volunteer who's in charge of mowing the yard.

This reality suggests that some orientation is task specific and needs to be done later, when the entire group isn't assembled. To force a bus driver to sit through a discussion about the proper cleaning of the communion cups is a waste of time—and guarantees the bus driver won't be back for more meetings.

There is some information every volunteer needs.
Where to park, what standards of conduct are expected, where the first aid kit is located—that's information that's universally needed.

This reality suggests that truly universal information is so important that it needs to be written down and accessible. A volunteer handbook and volunteer web site are two good places for this information to reside even after an orientation meeting.

There's some information you may not have.
You may have suspicions about what problems are most often encountered by new volunteers, but do you really know? You probably only hear about a fraction of the challenges faced by new volunteers; you're guessing about the rest.

This reality suggests that if you want to have a relevant orientation, you need to be asking volunteers to recommend what to include in the orientation. A survey of both current and new volunteers will provide agenda items.

And be sure that paid and unpaid staff who supervise volunteers have input, too. You want the orientation to meet their needs as well as the needs of the volunteers.

No matter what content you include, the initial meeting should be brief, relevant, and direct. Especially if you want volunteers to be back for more orientation, or ongoing training meetings, demonstrate that you can run a purposeful meeting that doesn't drag on forever.

Whatever else your orientation covers, these items are generally a good idea to include:

- The organizational chart (with no names listed next to titles)

- The church history, vision statement, and mission statement

- Your ministry's history, vision statement, and mission statement

- Training opportunities: who, what, when, where, why, and how

- Performance expectations and appraisal

- Safety information: evacuation plans, severe storm plans, and first aid kit location.

- Logistics: where to park, where to find the coffee pot, among others.

- And in every orientation meeting, be open for questions, comments, and observations from volunteers. Volunteers are absorbing information and assimilating into the culture; provide every opportunity for them to ask questions and get answers.

When Should You Schedule the Formal Orientation Program?

There's often a formal orientation event for new volunteers, an initial meeting where general information is shared and administrative matters are addressed. This has great value, as it helps volunteers assimilate quickly and easily.

But that initial event often results in a severe case of information overload. The new volunteer is inundated with details that can't possibly all be absorbed. Eyes glaze over. People fidget. So much data is pushed at volunteers that it's amazing any of it is retained at all.

A better solution is to give new volunteers less information, but to come back to talk with them several times. An initial meeting is worthwhile, but to avoid overload be careful to provide the right information at the right time.

> "Provide the right information at the right time."

At your initial meeting be certain to:

- Warmly, sincerely welcome new volunteers and ease their transition into new volunteer roles,

- Communicate essential information—but only essential information,

- Remind volunteers of the ministry's expectations about their conduct and contributions,

- Distribute and review any orientation handbooks that are needed by volunteers, and

- Offer to answer general questions that are of interest to everyone present. If a question is job-specific, respond to the interested volunteer after the meeting, or refer the volunteer to his or her ministry supervisor.

That's all you need to do at an initial, formal orientation meeting.

Is there more information volunteers need to know? Absolutely—but in a one-shot, group setting that's probably all anyone can take in. The rest of the material you can cover later in smaller groups organized around volunteer assignments, or in a one-on-one setting.

The fact is that at an orientation meeting volunteers probably don't yet know what they need to know. They won't have a clear picture of what's truly important information to master until they dive into their jobs and hit a few snags.

Remember the trip you won to Tuscany? You didn't know what you needed to know about Italian electrical current until you'd toasted your computer, or that walking is the standard mode of travel in small Tuscan villages until your toes were blistered and sore.

You learned from experience—and in some ways you want your orientation program to save your volunteers from a similar fate. Some things are great to learn from experience . . . but why make the same mistakes others have made?

Jim Wideman, a children's pastor who has more than a thousand volunteers involved in his program, says it well: "Experience is the best teacher . . . but it doesn't have to be *your* experience."

> "Effective orientation is an ongoing process."

The secret of an effective orientation program doesn't lie in hosting a tremendous formal meeting anyway. It's this: Effective orientation is an ongoing process. You can't hold one orientation meeting and then cross it off your list forever.

Remember: The purpose of orientation is to answer the question, "What's it like to live or work here?" Every time a volunteer changes jobs, or the job the volunteer is doing changes, or the culture or rules change—it's time for more orientation. The process never actually stops. Never.

Who Should Lead the Orientation Program and Process?

At the risk of sounding ungrateful, let us suggest that you may not be the best candidate for the job.

Not that you haven't done great work in connecting the new volunteers with appropriate service opportunities. And not that you wouldn't do a stellar job of facilitating the orientation. After all, you're probably the one who pulled the information together.

But you probably aren't the person who will be supervising the volunteers, or being in a primary relationship with them. If you have enough volunteers entering into a particular area of ministry, it's a good idea to let the person who will be supervising them do the orientation.

Of course, maybe the new crop of volunteers will report to you, or your volunteer ministry is small enough that you can be in relationship with everyone. If that's the case, go to it. Lead the orientation program yourself—but still involve others in the overall process.

And have people who will be working with the volunteers at the formal orientation. From the very start you can help volunteers find buddies who know the ropes, who serve in the ministry roles in which the new volunteers will serve.

> "Have people who will be working with the volunteers at the formal orientation."

A case study: the Group Workcamps orientation program.

Each summer, Group Workcamps organizes more than 60 week-long, short-term mission programs where teenagers repair homes of the elderly and disadvantaged. The vast majority of the leaders at those Workcamps—each of which is housed in a community school and involves an average of 350 teenagers and youth leaders—are volunteers.

More than a thousand volunteers are needed each summer, and because of the program's reputation and excellence, each year that number of volunteers is recruited, screened, placed, and trained. Workcamp volunteers do everything from manage the school kitchens, to coordinate travel, to work alongside teenagers as together they roof a house or paint a porch.

Note the scope of this volunteer program—it's huge. The Workcamps themselves are scattered in communities all over the continent. There are more than a dozen volunteer roles at each camp, and one of the more challenging is the job of "director."

Directors are the people ultimately responsible for running the Workcamps. If a youth leader falls through a ceiling, or the food vendor fails to deliver the lettuce, or a teenager drifts away from a worksite, the director gets involved.

Because of the complexity of preparing for the role, there's an orientation for Workcamp directors in Colorado each May. Volunteers who will direct camps are flown in, housed at a YMCA high in the Rockies, and given three days of orientation and training.

And during those three days, what do you think is the single most energetically received session?

It's this: a several-hour meeting where new directors get the opportunity to ask veteran directors what to expect. There's no agenda other than to connect first-time volunteers with people who've dealt with the same responsibilities before.

> "The orientation is relational, not agenda-driven."

The orientation is relational, not agenda-driven, and relationships that form continue through e-mails, phone calls, and encouraging notes between peers. The session sets an expectation that directors will be helpful to each other and responsive when there's a question or concern.

The inch-thick orientation and training manual every director receives is packed with helpful information. It's useful. It's referred to often. It's practical and well organized.

But the manual isn't the magic.

Something else happens during that three-day orientation and training meeting that shapes volunteers into directors who will embrace a week-long Workcamp experience that keeps them up into the wee hours of the morning day after day. That requires them to be servants even if they're tired. That inspires them to deliver top-flight customer service to teenagers and youth leaders alike.

Here's what happens during those three days that makes the difference—and you can reap similar rewards if you can build these elements into your orientation program, too . . .

Volunteers are immersed in Workcamp culture.

The staff hosting the orientation doesn't just talk about serving others; they model it in a hundred ways to the new volunteers. Meetings start and end promptly. Questions are answered clearly. Requested information is tracked down and reported. The needs of volunteers are taken seriously—which is exactly what will be expected of the directors when they're running their own camps.

For three solid days, the Group Workcamp vision, mission, and values are soaked up by volunteers.

Anything that will be expected of directors at their Workcamps is modeled during the orientation. That way there's never a question as to what's meant by "service" or "leadership." Everyone has experienced it.

Top people lead the orientation program.

When the Senior Pastor or CEO shows up to lead an orientation session, that communicates the significance of the orientation process. At the Group Workcamp orientation new volunteers hear from—and have dinner with—the founder of the program. And the people leading sessions are front-line staff.

Be sure you have your best people leading your orientation programs, too. And having your Senior Pastor show up to personally thank your volunteers for their commitment and servant hearts will fire up your team.

Stories are shared.

There's power in stories. The stories we share carry the DNA of our values and culture. The stories highlight what's important and lift up heroes to emulate.

> "There's power in stories."

At the Group Workcamp orientation, stories play a central role. They're told to illustrate what works—and doesn't work. What's wise—and what's foolish. What matters—and what's not important. Stories are shared with humor and laughter, but never is the point missed: There's truth in these stories. Let those with ears hear and understand.

In your orientation process, tell the story of how your volunteer ministry came into being. In the process you'll share what vision motivated your founders to persevere until the ministry was born. Tell stories about volunteers who've made you proud—they embody the attributes that are considered virtues in your culture.

And never miss the opportunity to capture stories as they unfold in your ministry. The best stories you could tell next year may well be happening right now.

New volunteers are celebrated.

There's always a temptation for veterans to form cliques. It's just natural: They're friends who've shared experiences, and perhaps they seldom see each other between annual orientation sessions.

Although it's natural, it's toxic for new volunteers.

At the Group Workcamp orientation, newcomers are intentionally integrated into sessions with veteran volunteers. Past experience is applauded and appreciated, but in many ways it's irrelevant. The focus is preparing for the summer ahead, not reminiscing about past Workcamps. New volunteers are given high honor for their willingness to serve and celebrated as legitimate members of the team.

How do you handle cliques among your volunteers—especially among groups of long-term volunteers? Where is there an opportunity for newcomers to be heard, accepted, and endorsed?

Evaluations are filled out.

How do you know what's preparing your volunteers for their roles and what's not helping? You ask your volunteers. They know—at least, the experienced volunteers know.

Don't let a formal orientation program in your church go past without designing in an evaluation of the program and the process. For your convenience, a Program Evaluation Form is on page 100. Adapt it to use at your formal orientation programs. You'll also be asking volunteers to fill out the same form after three to six months; comparing their answers will let you know what they remember and what was most and least helpful.

You probably won't be flying your volunteers to a remote mountain getaway for three days anytime soon. But you can pull together a one-day retreat . . . or even a half-day retreat. It's a chance for you to transform volunteers into servants who will rise above even their own expectations.

TWO
The Volunteer Orientation Staff Handbook

Most companies provide a handbook to staff members during orientation—and you should, too. Here's why ... and what you need to include.

Denise's first day at her new job wasn't quite what she expected.

"First we had a tour of the facility," she reports. "I saw where I'd be sitting, and figured out where to hang my coat and stash my purse. I had lunch with one of the people on my team. That stuff I pretty much knew was coming."

What took Denise by surprise was how she spent the afternoon.

"Six of us sat in a little conference room for three hours," she says in amazement. "We opened up an employee handbook and took turns reading through it—out loud. Then we had to sign a form that said we'd read the handbook. I was bored out of my mind."

Denise shakes her head as she remembers what felt like a wasted afternoon. "I just can't believe that was the best use of our time. We had a million things we could have done, and they had us reading out loud like we were in first grade. Somebody must really care about that handbook," she says.

It probably was the best use of Denise's time to read through the handbook. While the presentation style was at best mind-numbing, it did expose Denise and the other new hires to critical information they need to know.

And because everyone walked out of the conference room with a copy of the handbook, Denise knows where to find the details she's forgotten when she's wondering how to schedule vacation time or wondering what the company's policy is about snow days.

But that's a for-profit company. They need orientation handbooks for new hires, right? Does your volunteer ministry really require you to create one?

Yes . . . and here's why.

Five Reasons You Need a Volunteer Ministry Orientation Handbook

Creating a handbook can be a time-consuming task, even if you start with another church's handbook as a model. But without question developing a handbook is worth the investment—for at least five reasons:

1. **Orientation handbooks compensate for information overload.**

Volunteers can absorb just so much information at a time. Trying to cram too many policies and procedures into their heads at one time is like continuing to pour milk into a glass that's already full: There's no more room.

A handbook provides the details in a handy reference guide. The volunteer may not recall exactly what the policy is about appropriate clothing, but she knows where to look it up.

2. **Orientation handbooks are open 24/7.**

Who are the volunteers going to call if they can't remember the procedure for lining up a substitute Sunday school teacher? You—of course. Do you really want that to happen again and again?

If you've outlined the procedure in a handbook, volunteers can find the needed information anytime . . . without phoning you at 10:30 on a Saturday night. A well-written, clear handbook intercepts and answers many questions before they reach you.

3. Orientation handbooks are empowering.

Giving volunteers information in written form empowers them to make many decisions without having to ask for information. They'll know the church's philosophy of discipline and how they'll be reviewed.

4. Orientation handbooks require you to set policies.

Orientation handbooks force you—and other ministry leaders—to think through policies and procedures that affect volunteers. What should volunteers do if a tornado warning sounds while they're working with children at church? What are appropriate boundaries to respect in the adult-teenager mentoring program? How will volunteers be evaluated?

You can't write policies until you've made hard decisions about how situations should generally be handled, and that often takes some discussion among church leaders. But that's a good thing: The time and energy you invest in creating policies is time and energy volunteers don't have to exert wondering what to do when situations arise.

By the way, if you're a member of Group's Church Volunteer Central, visit www.churchvolunteercentral.com for examples of brief, clear policies. Not a member of Group's Church Volunteer Central? Call 1-800-447-1070 for information about what it can do for you and your volunteer ministry.

5. Orientation handbooks establish expectations.

If you expect volunteers to uphold standards, you've got to make clear what those standards are. If you don't want to see gossip, have a conflict resolution system established. If you expect all volunteers to attend worship services regularly, say so.

> "If you expect something of paid staff, expect it from unpaid staff, too."

And a word about standards: If you expect something of paid staff, expect it from unpaid staff, too. It's a double standard to insist that no staff members smoke on church property, but then put out ashtrays for volunteers. Hold everyone to the same high standards. Doing less will confuse church members who don't see all that much difference between the Associate Pastor of Christian Education (a paid staff position) and the Sunday School Superintendent (an unpaid staff position).

Besides, when you expect less of unpaid staff than paid staff, you demean your volunteers. Treat them like professionals, too.

So you need a volunteer handbook. Does that mean you have to have it ready for that first, formal orientation meeting? And do you really have to sit there and read it out loud?

The fact is that reading a long list of policies to volunteers accomplishes little. Volunteers won't remember what you said, and the policies won't impact their behavior. It's largely a waste of time if you're trying to teach volunteers information.

"Everyone knows this stuff counts."

But here's what it does accomplish (and even our friend Denise noticed it on her first day at the new job): *When you stop and read the handbook it communicates how very important the material in the handbook is to the organization—and to the new volunteer or employee.* You draw attention to it. You shine a spotlight on it. And everyone knows that no matter what, this stuff counts.

Many companies and churches don't go to the lengths Denise's company did—they don't expect employees to read handbook policies aloud. Instead, they distribute handbooks and set a deadline by which employees must return a form stating the handbook has been read.

We'd like to suggest you adapt that procedure slightly. Distribute handbooks at your first formal orientation meeting. Also distribute a Volunteer Handbook Acknowledgement Form (page 99) that volunteers must sign and return before they're allowed to serve in their volunteer role.

But what if you're a small church? Everyone knows everyone, and it's easy to explain to people how things work and what to do. Why bother with creating a handbook full of policies everyone already knows?

Even if you're in a church of 50 members, your volunteer ministry needs written policies in a handbook. Here's why . . .

- **Policies help resolve problems and eliminate hazards.**

A friend of ours is a lifeguard at a city pool. When he was hired he thought his job would be to sit on a platform diligently watching the water, ever prepared to toss aside his whistle and clipboard and dive in to drag out a drowning swimmer.

His supervisor straightened the young man out.

"Your job is first and foremost not to rescue people who are victims of accidents or stupidity," the supervisor said. "Your job is to keep people from having accidents or doing anything stupid."

During the course of his summer the young man never once dove in to save someone. But more times than he could count he kept children from running on the slick cement around the pool and enforced rules that kept weak swimmers out of the deep water. The lifeguard discovered that the pool policies he'd at first thought were silly actually kept people safe.

Your volunteer ministry policies can accomplish the same thing: Keep volunteers from getting into deep water without realizing it.

It may seem like a perfectly logical thing for Jack Smith to drop off a couple kids from the youth group after the meeting, and since Alisa's house is near his it just stands to reason Jack will take Alisa, a 17-year-old girl, home last.

> "Your volunteer ministry policies can keep volunteers from getting into deep water."

So there Jack is in the car at night, alone with a high school junior. Not smart.

A written policy about never having an adult with a minor in a car alone could have prevented Jack from ever making this mistake by setting a boundary beyond which he couldn't go.

- **Policies clarify responsibilities.**

Knowing who is responsible to make decisions when the roof leaks is a good thing for the Sunday school teacher who stops by the building on a Saturday afternoon to pick up curriculum and notices an inch of water in the church basement.

If your volunteer handbook doesn't have a page titled, "Who You Gonna Call?" add one—fast. But do it by the title of the person responsible, not the name. When the Sunday school teacher sees she should call the "building and grounds deacon," she can then check the phone list to see who that is. Remember: Keeping the phone list and the handbook separate saves you from having to constantly update the handbook when people fill new roles or phone numbers change.

- **Policies provide stability and continuity.**

Over the course of a few years you may have a complete turnover in volunteer staff in some area of ministry. You'll still be able to deliver a consistent level of service if everyone is on the same page concerning expectations—and the policies in your volunteer handbook can deliver those expectations.

- **Handbooks will help you provide a thorough orientation.**

Encourage volunteers to highlight items as they read through their handbooks. Then, at your next team meeting, discuss the policies—answering questions and highlighting the policies that you think are most important.

You'll be able to move through the material more quickly if everyone has read the handbook, and you'll know if something in the handbook is unclear because those are the sections that will generate the most questions.

Be sure volunteers write their names in their handbooks, too. Be clear that every volunteer is to have a copy of the handbook, to read it, and to affirm that he or she has read the entire document.

And make sure you keep track of who's read the handbook. You'll need that information when it's time to update or add a policy and issue a new handbook or replace selected pages in handbooks.

Also, your insurance company may offer discounts on liability coverage if you can demonstrate that no volunteer is placed until after having read policies about issues like child safety, sexual harassment, and confidentiality. Check with your insurance provider to see if any such discount is available to you.

When volunteers turn in their Volunteer Handbook Acknowledgment Form, keep the signed forms in their files. This documentation may be helpful should your church ever face civil litigation.

Feel free to adapt the Volunteer Handbook Acknowledgment Form to fit your unique situation. It's merely a template; have it reviewed by your legal counsel and make whatever changes are appropriate. Also, be mindful a signed form may have no impact whatsoever in the case of litigation . . . but it is one way to prove you attempted to communicate important policies.

Still not convinced? Then think about this . . .

• **Policies make managing a program easier.**

Because policies include the "what," often the "why," and occasionally the "how" of a decision, you don't have to rethink situations each time they arise. Some of that has already been done and formalized; you can simply determine if circumstances warrant making an exception.

Look—every volunteer ministry makes policy decisions frequently. They just don't call them "policy decisions" or write them down. It may be that your developing policies is as easy as reviewing the decisions your leadership has made lately, and getting those decisions down on paper. One example of how that might look is on page 107. It's a list of policies related to the nursery at First Christian Church—see how many decisions have been captured in simple policy statements.

Be proactive, too. Lots of policies are developed because

something has gone wrong and nobody wants it to happen again. So do this: Think about what might reasonably be expected to go wrong and decide how you'll handle it now—before the bus breaks down, the power goes out, or the hurricane hits. Put your plan in writing.

Your handbook of policies won't be an imposition on your volunteers. In fact, your volunteers will welcome having the clarity and reassurance of the handbook.

Types of Policies

A word about policies before you begin writing them for your handbook: Policies are not all created equal. Some are non-negotiable, and others are very negotiable. Let's take a look at both categories.

> "You need to always be meeting or exceeding the requirements of the law."

Non-negotiable policies

Some policies reflect local or federal laws. That you're working with volunteers rather than paid staff, or operating in a church rather than a company, doesn't change the law. It's real—and you need to always be meeting or exceeding the requirements of the law.

In Romans 13 we read,

Everyone must submit himself to the governing authorities, for there is no authority except that which God has established. The authorities that exist have been established by God. Consequently, he who rebels against the authority is rebelling against what God has instituted, and those who do so will bring judgment on themselves. (Romans 13:1-2)

If local building codes require you to not have more than 120 people in a room, don't let the 121st person through the door. If the Health Department insists you maintain your church kitchen at a certain level of cleanliness because you serve meals to the homeless twice per week, amaze the Health Inspector with how the floor sparkles and the food preparation meets every requirement.

And if federal law says you shouldn't sexually harass someone, don't do it. Ever. Period.

In some cases churches are able to bypass or be exempted from statutes that apply elsewhere—but why would you want to not measure up? If civil policies are about respecting the rights and dignity of people, be very, very careful about deciding they don't apply to you.

When you create your handbook and review it with volunteers, be clear that non-negotiable policies are just that: non-negotiable. Breaking them will result in being separated from volunteer opportunities in the church at minimum, and in some cases civil prosecution.

Negotiable policies

Some policies are simply principles you've put in place to guide action. They're not laws. They can be bent or broken without dramatic consequences.

For instance, if your policy is to have Sunday school teachers sign on for six-month terms of service, that's a decision you've already made. You might have created that policy to help ensure consistency for the children in the Sunday school.

But if a woman who's taught Sunday school for just four months were to suddenly lose her husband, you wouldn't try to force her to complete her term of service. You could easily make an exception—and probably should make an exception.

The point: These policies are set in wet cement. Exceptions can be made, but be judicious about how often and for what reasons you make exceptions. In general, make exceptions rarely and only for good cause. A policy that's not applied fairly and consistently will quickly become a point of conflict.

Here are categories of negotiable policies you'll want to include in your handbook:

How-to-get-things-done policies

These policies concern themselves with how tasks are completed. For example, the volunteer serving as the church secretary will undoubtedly get phone calls—and those calls need to be handled professionally. One policy you might put in place for your entire volunteer ministry is that every phone call, e-mail, or other message must be responded to within 24 hours.

If the volunteer serving in the church office happens to miss the mark and returns a call two days late, will the volunteer be fired? No—but it will be cause for a discussion and review of the job expectation so the volunteer understands the importance of the policy.

When-to-get-things-done policies

If your volunteers are reimbursed for expenses, someone in the accounting office wants those expense reports on time so he or she can close out the month.

Don't expect volunteers to have the same sense of urgency about your deadlines that you have—unless you tell them those deadlines are important.

What-to-do-and-not-do policies

These policies explain what volunteers can and cannot do. They set boundaries that help define what appropriate relationships look like.

These policies may be negotiable or non-negotiable; it depends on what boundary will be crossed.

A negotiable policy may involve whether a Sunday school teacher can buy a child a birthday present. The answer: Certainly—but only if it's small, and only if it's something the teacher does for every child in his class.

These policies may also identify a boundary that a volunteer cannot cross, such as "borrowing" offering money as a short-term loan, or inviting a student to go on a date. Crossing that sort of boundary elevates the issue to a non-negotiable policy.

What Should Be in Your Volunteer Orientation Handbook?

First, here's what *shouldn't* be there . . .

- Don't include organizational charts with names attached, phone lists, or anything else that's likely to need frequent updating. Ideally, you'll make changes in the handbook infrequently, and only when there's an addition or change in policies.

- Don't include anything that you don't intend to enforce. Companies have found that if they're lax about enforcing one part of an employee handbook (drug testing, for instance) then employees can be justified in assuming that other policies (taking unannounced vacations, for example) won't be enforced, either. You won't find yourself in court trying to fire volunteers because they didn't give two weeks' notice before heading off to Montana to go elk hunting, but the principle has merit. If you aren't going to take something in your handbook seriously, don't include it.

- Don't include the little stuff. If your pet peeve is when nursery workers forget to empty the diaper pail on Sundays, the place to deal with that is in a training session with nursery workers. Don't add a separate section in the handbook about WHAT TO DO WITH STINKY STUFF. Use your handbook to focus on the larger, more general issues.

> "Anything vague or cute should be cut."

- Anything vague or cute should be cut from your handbook. Humor is fine, and if it's part of your culture and you encourage it, you'll want to let it shine through. But don't let humor or cuteness interfere with the clarity of your handbook. Write to ensure you're not misunderstood. Use crisp, definite language. Say what you mean.

- Any specifics that are covered in job descriptions. Keep things simple: Let job descriptions speak for themselves.

That's what shouldn't clutter up a handbook.

But what should be in a handbook? And how do you keep your handbook from becoming a 300-page manual that few can lift and no one will read?

You'll greatly increase the value of your handbook if you use it to communicate the information that doesn't change—and you communicate the information briefly.

That is, you don't need to deliver the last word on who brings the donuts on Sunday mornings, and how you really should bring a variety that includes cream filled, nut covered, glazed, and also plain donuts; that a box of glazed donuts might be easy but will fail to please some of the teachers—and you can probably guess which ones they are, isn't it obvious?—and, by the way, don't forget the cinnamon twists: They're the director's favorites.

Just say snacks are available in the teachers' prep room on Sundays. Be brief. Be clear.

Here are eleven areas you should address in your policy handbook. They're in no particular order; they're all important.

1. Your ministry's mission, vision, and values

Include the mission statement, vision statement, and a brief description of what you value. Be sure what you include is consistent with your overall church's values, mission, and vision.

If your ministry places a special emphasis on teamwork, communication, diversity, quality, or another value, briefly define that value and describe what it looks like in your setting.

2. The general organizational structure of your ministry

Without naming names, describe who reports to whom. This is your chance to proactively re-route most phone calls away from yourself, so be thorough!

Provide the organizational chart here; the easily updated phone list you hand out with the handbook will supply the details. You did remember to identify each person on your phone list by ministry role, too, didn't you? If not, add that information. It doesn't help if in the handbook you instruct teachers to call their section supervisors as identified on the phone list and then the phone list doesn't say who does what.

3. Dress codes and other behavior standards

If staff members aren't to use tobacco or alcohol while serving a term as a volunteer, say so. If that prohibition extends only to the times volunteers are actually serving, say that instead. Be clear where you can be, especially on behaviors that are black and white, done or not done.

Some of those standards may be abundantly clear, such as . . .

- No pierced body parts visible (other than simple earrings),

- No visible tattoos, and

- No fad clothing (for example, grunge or gothic).

It's trickier when the behaviors involve interpretation, such as what constitutes "modest" apparel. Imprecise terms such as "modestly" and "professionally" leave a lot of gray area.

How high can a skirt go and still be modest? How tight can jeans be and still be professional? Who decides if someone has violated the policy, and who's going to tell the offender? How should it be resolved?

Your policy isn't the place to nit-pick about the number of inches a hemline can rise above the knee, or precisely what a T-shirt slogan can or can't say. Your goal isn't to create a comprehensive rulebook, but to briefly communicate standards.

Most volunteers are ready and eager to cheerfully comply with standards—once the standards are clear. So if you use vague words, supply a couple of examples of what you mean. Volunteers will get the message.

And here's a tip: Should someone show up to teach in clothing that's inappropriate, ask a leader of the same sex to take the offender aside and calmly suggest that the individual change clothes and then return to the volunteer role. Be careful not to communicate condemnation or spiritual superiority, but instead a gentle, caring redirection to what "modest" means in the context of the volunteer setting.

4. Equipment and facility usage

Is it okay to use the church's copier to make a copy of your son's social studies report? Is it okay to use the computer in the accounting office to look up possible condo rentals in Vail for next winter? to look up stock prices? to look up porno sites?

What exactly are your policies regarding the use of the church's equipment and facilities? Your handbook is a great place to explain them.

5. The performance evaluation system

When and how do you evaluate volunteers? Describe the process so there are no surprises later. Having this spelled out is reassuring to volunteers because it communicates you care enough to actually come see what they're doing and to help them improve. A performance evaluation system says you value them and their work.

6. Safety information

Include evacuation plans, severe storm plans, the location of first aid kits, and a notification system to use in case someone is hurt. Be especially brief here; when there's blood on the floor the average person will remember just one or two things, not a complex maze of instructions.

And don't forget to include standards about the situations in which adults can be with teenagers or children. What seems harmless at the time can take on sinister tones when viewed under the harsh light of a police inquiry or the direct questions of parents. Your policies can keep volunteers from getting themselves into trouble.

7. Security information

Do children need to be checked in and out? What's your system for that? Must outside doors be secured in some areas? Who has permission to activate or deactivate an alarm system? Spell out—briefly and clearly—what principles and standards you're maintaining in the effort to keep people secure.

Include a statement about which positions require background or police record checks and never, ever fail to enforce this policy. List what other screening, training, and supervision your church provides, too. And include a church policy statement on confidentiality and privacy.

8. Logistics

Are volunteers to park in a certain spot so visitors can have the closest parking spots? Is there a specific system for reserving audio-visual equipment or getting a broken chair repaired? Where are mops and buckets kept? A brief review of this information will help volunteers fit into the church's procedures.

9. Grievance procedures

Not everything will go smoothly 100 percent of the time. When a volunteer feels he or she has a legitimate complaint against a supervisor, what should the volunteer do?

Jesus provides some excellent guidelines for conflict resolution in the book of Matthew.

Consider . . .

> But I tell you that anyone who is angry with his brother will be subject to judgment. Again, anyone who says to his brother, "Raca," is answerable to the Sanhedrin. But anyone who says, "You fool!" will be in danger of the fire of hell. Therefore, if you are offering your gift at the altar and there remember that your brother has something against you, leave your gift there in front of the altar. First go and be reconciled to your brother; then come and offer your gift. (Matthew 5:22-23)

> But I tell you: Love your enemies and pray for those who persecute you. (Matthew 5:44)

> If your brother sins against you, go and show him his fault, just between the two of you. If he listens to you, you have won your brother over. But if he will not listen, take one or two others along, so that "every matter may be established by the testimony of two or three witnesses." If he refuses to listen to them, tell it to the church; and if he refuses to listen even to the church, treat him as you would a pagan or a tax collector. (Matthew 18:15-17)

In short: Forgive, confront, seek resolution. It's a good idea to apply those principles to your situation if there's dissent in the ranks. If your policy about conflict specifies that volunteers should talk first to someone who can actually do something to resolve the situation, you'll eliminate a great deal of gossip.

10. Career development opportunities

Volunteers have careers, too. Some volunteers have several of them—one inside the church, and one outside the walls of your building.

> "In short: Forgive, confront, seek resolution."

Take Eddie for instance. On Sunday morning he's an adult class leader, taking a group of parents through a study of good parenting habits. But on Monday morning he's a medical doctor explaining to patients why they should exercise.

Eddie has two careers—one as a teacher and one as a doctor—and he wants to grow in both of them.

What opportunities can you offer Eddie that will help him grow? A master teacher mentor who will assess his teaching and facilitating skills? That will help Eddie in both his careers, so you'll find him eager to sign on.

If you can offer mentoring, training courses, a library of useful training materials, or any other development opportunities, tell volunteers about them.

11. Scheduled events and activities

Do you have quarterly training meetings? an annual banquet? staff meetings on Sunday mornings? If you have regular programming, identify it and be clear about whether attendance is encouraged, optional, or mandatory.

Handbooks Are Not All That's Needed

Don't think distributing a handbook of policies completes the orientation process. Handbooks are helpful—but they aren't the last word in orientation.

In addition to orienting new volunteers, be sure to let existing volunteers who will work alongside the new faces know that someone is coming. Make introductions, and encourage existing volunteers to connect with new people over a cup of coffee or a donut.

Informal orientation will happen only if volunteer peers are talking. True, you don't know what the veteran volunteers might say, but they'll say it anyway—you might as well encourage the process.

Also, see that the paid or unpaid staff members who will supervise the new volunteers quickly arrange individual meetings with their new reports. The relationship volunteers have with their supervisors will make or break the volunteers' experience. It's the supervisors who will shape the volunteers' work flow and are positioned to best provide training and encouragement.

Some churches have found it helpful to create a video that includes orientation material. If done well, this can be a benefit—but it shouldn't (and can't) replace person-to-person contact.

Finally, arrange for a follow-up program in three to six months. Get the same group of volunteers back together for a "reunion" and see how they're doing in their roles. If you're in a large church it's possible they haven't talked since their formal orientation program. They'll enjoy seeing each other again and swapping stories, and you'll have the chance to administer the same test you gave them after the first orientation program.

Compare test scores and comments. You may find that something the new volunteers rated poorly on their first test is ranked highly on the second test. Use what you learn to shape future orientation programs and processes.

And here's a challenge for you to consider taking: When you've completed your orientation process, give each volunteer a copy of the Volunteer Bill of Rights you'll find on page 110. It summarizes the basic expectations volunteers should see met. Are you delivering them? Some have to do with orientation and training, some with the design of your volunteer ministry.

Transition to Training

The formal orientation program covers the big picture issues, but most of your volunteers' questions will be about their specific tasks. You probably aren't prepared to answer those questions; that's up to the volunteers' supervisors.

We'll focus on training next, and it's a piece of the puzzle that you'll find challenges you like few other areas of volunteer leadership. Training requires you to set aside your preconceptions and do a great deal of listening well before you ever begin talking.

THREE
Training Volunteers

The benefits of providing training—for you, your church, and your volunteers. Plus a great story about a hospital you won't want to visit anytime soon.

The administrator at a large hospital in the Midwest had a problem.

The hospital's maternity unit was bursting at the seams—thousands of women gave birth at the hospital each year. Business was booming, and referrals were at an all-time high. Beds were constantly full, and the nursery was constantly packed with babies.

That wasn't the problem.

The problem, the administrator nervously admitted to a researcher, was the orientation program hosted by the hospital on the first Thursday of each month. It had been organized for nearly ten years by the maternity floor Head Nurse and her assistants, and hundreds of women and their partners filled the hospital auditorium each month to be oriented about how to have a baby at the hospital.

The information was clear: what door to come in, how to fill out paperwork, what the visiting hours were, where cars could be parked after dropping off the women in labor. The audience even got a tour of the Maternity Unit, including a peek at the newborns in the nursery. And everyone left with a bag piled high with sample packs of diapers, formula, and wipes. Some lucky moms won door prizes that included new car seats and other expensive baby gear.

The problem, said the hospital administrator, was that in spite of the orientation program the admission procedure for women in labor was chaotic at best. Nobody knew how to fill out the forms or could remember which elevator took them straight to the Maternity Unit. There was no discernable difference between patients who had attended the orientation and those who hadn't.

> "The orientation was expensive, but was it working?"

The orientation was expensive, but was it working? Should it be expanded? modified? dropped altogether?

And to further complicate matters, the Head Nurse was convinced that her orientation program was the only thing keeping anarchy from breaking out on the Maternity Unit. When the administrator inquired about tweaking the program, she'd announced she had no intention of changing one word of what she considered to be a perfect program. Case closed.

So evaluating the orientation program had to happen very, very delicately.

Six weeks and a hundred interviews later, here's what was discovered: The women and partners who presented themselves at the hospital doors wanted to know just two things . . .

What's the fastest way to the Maternity Unit? Patients knew there was a dedicated elevator, but in the grips of contractions nobody could remember where it was. Nor did they care. They wanted someone—anyone—to personally escort them where they needed to go.

How can I get painkillers? Enough with the small talk and forms. Where's the anesthesiologist?

The problem with the hospital's orientation program was that it centered on what the hospital wanted people to know. It answered questions patients weren't asking. It covered material patients ultimately decided was unimportant.

Patients didn't care if it was inconvenient when they left their cars parked on the sidewalk by the emergency room entrance. Patients didn't care if forms had to be filled out singly or in triplicate. Those are things that mattered to the hospital, not the patients.

The researcher suggested that a team of volunteers should provide escorts and valet parking services to supplement or replace the orientation program. Satisfaction with the hospital would rise, and the cost of the orientation could potentially disappear.

The suggestion was never implemented.

Notice that the hospital was doing good things. The nurses stayed late once each month to meet with expectant moms and their partners—that's a good thing. They convinced hospital vendors to donate sample packs of baby stuff—that's a good thing, too. The nurses gave tours and handed out flyers and brochures by the dozen—and that's a good thing.

But they missed the mark.

Why? Because the hospital staff didn't start by identifying what the patients wanted to know.

The patients wanted to know the bare minimum a panicked person can retain about how to get to a doctor and an epidural. From the patient's perspective, that was the training material that mattered. Everything else was irrelevant.

If there's a moral to this story it would be this: Good intentions aren't enough when it comes to training. It requires careful attention to what's really needed—and not just from your perspective.

"Good intentions aren't enough when it comes to training."

The Cost of Training

We couldn't track down who said it first, but we spotted the saying on a bumper sticker: "If you think education is expensive, try ignorance."

It's true, isn't it? Education is expensive. Educating your

volunteers through carefully designed training sessions is expensive—but consider what it costs if you let them operate in the dark.

- What might happen if a nursery attendant doesn't understand the proper ways to provide security for babies?

- What might happen if an elementary teacher doesn't know how to apply loving correction?

- What might happen if a youth volunteer doesn't see anything wrong with letting the kids go unchaperoned at the youth lock-in?

- What might happen if someone ushering thinks nobody will notice if he slips away from his post to grab a cup of coffee with friends over in the Hospitality Café?

- What might happen if . . . ?

Clearly ignorance is not bliss—not when it comes to working with volunteers.

Why Training Is Worth the Effort—and Cost

It's how you build in excellence.

When you embrace the idea of training, you get to decide how excellent your programming will be. If you don't do training, you take what you can get.

Think about it: If you've placed appropriate people in volunteer roles, you know they're capable. There's at least a good chance they can accomplish the job set before them.

And they're motivated—they signed up, went through interviewing and placement, and completed orientation. They want to deliver great service.

But there's a lot they don't know, and in any volunteer role what you don't know can hurt you—or at least hurt your performance. Your volunteers will stumble along doing their best, but it's completely possible for them to make the same mistake over and over again—because they don't know any better.

If you want excellence, training is worth the effort.

It's how you make volunteers happy.

Training is also worth the effort if you're looking for happy volunteers.

Nobody likes feeling incompetent, especially when the job is important. To you a volunteer stuffing inserts into bulletins may not look like he's doing anything complicated, but you're wrong. He's given up a morning with his wife to be at the church, sitting in a corner of the office, sticking pieces of paper inside a bulletin cover. His back is acting up because he's sardined at a table that isn't really comfortable, but he's not complaining. He's praying for the people who will receive the bulletins on Sunday morning.

He's not doing grunt work. He's doing ministry.

So imagine how happy he'll be if, as he wraps up the 500th bulletin cover, you point out that the yellow insert should have gone in before the brown one.

Want happy volunteers? Training is worth the effort.

It's how you hold down costs.

True, training volunteers can be expensive in terms of preparation time and photocopies. But imagine what it would cost if you had to hire professionals to do everything volunteers do?

People wiser than us have pointed out that if you want to do a job in the most cost-effective way, you need to clearly understand what you're trying to accomplish before you get started and decide how you'll proceed. That's true with building highways, and it's true with trimming the church lawn.

Don't let people learn from trial and error. You'll pay for each error.

Want to hold down costs? Training is worth the effort.

It's how you respect the calling of volunteers.

If you truly believe that God brings volunteers into ministry roles so they can grow closer to him and use their spiritual gifts, abilities, skills, and passions, your job is to help them. You'll want to encourage and equip them. And that means providing training opportunities so they get ever more capable in service.

Want to cooperate with God's purposes? Training is worth the effort.

There's no reason to fail to provide training, just excuses.

If you're directing the volunteer ministry in your church, you'll find yourself in the role of "trainer." You may be training volunteers who report directly to you, or training other ministry leaders how to train the volunteers who report to them. However your church ministries are configured, training will play a significant role in them.

Let's consider your role of trainer.

Trainers—What Do They Do, Exactly?

If your mental image of a trainer is someone who's standing in front of a room, holding a clipboard and speaking to rows of attentive learners, you've got some challenges ahead of you.

That view of training—the expert lecturing students—is both out of date and ultimately ineffective.

Here's the thing: There are talented people who make careers out of becoming ever more expert trainers. They study how people learn, and how to set up environments where adults are best able to focus and retain knowledge. They study learning styles, presentation styles, and what tools can bridge the two. Every day they study what works, what doesn't work, and what could work better.

> "Don't worry— you're up to the challenge."

And to think: Training is just one of the hats you have to wear!

Don't worry—you're up to the challenge. Training, at heart, is teaching—and if you're like most volunteer ministry leaders you've had considerable experience helping others learn new information and build new skills.

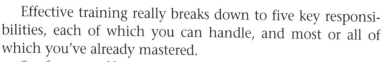

Effective training really breaks down to five key responsibilities, each of which you can handle, and most or all of which you've already mastered.

See for yourself:

Responsibility 1: Prepare and prepare some more.

The first place you'll do preparation is the training material itself.

We'll dig into how to develop appropriate content for training sessions later in this volume, but for now realize that effective training takes considerable effort and focus. It's not something you throw together at the last minute.

Plus, you need to prepare the volunteers themselves. In the sessions you lead you'll put them at ease and share why the training they'll experience is important. As a trainer it's your job to capture the volunteers' attention; don't assume they'll just give it to you. It's your job to create (and maintain) a compelling learning environment.

Responsibility 2: Explain the skill or task you're addressing in training.

Let's say you're showing office volunteers how to operate the photocopy machine. The volunteers are responsible for creating, designing, and copying flyers for an upcoming event. Operating "Ol' Jambox" (as your antiquated machine is affectionately known) is a skill they'll need.

The trick is for you to break down the information into manageable bites and build on information the volunteers already have.

Responsibility 3: Show as well as tell.

It's one thing to hear about how to do a task, and another to see it demonstrated. Help volunteers grasp how to operate the office photocopy machine by actually pulling open drawers and pushing buttons. Show volunteers where the paper goes in, where it comes out, and how to find the fire extinguisher if Ol' Jambox decides to burst into flames—again.

Responsibility 4: Involve volunteers in actually doing the task or skill.

Volunteers' confidence grows when they have the opportunity to perform the tasks or practice using the skill while you're there to coach them through it. A trainer learns to monitor closely at first, then gradually step back as volunteers develop competence and good habits. You'll help volunteers process their newfound information as they work with the copier.

Responsibility 5: Review and retrain.

As volunteers operate Ol' Jambox, give them encouragement and honest feedback. Maybe one of the volunteers seems to have a feel for communicating with the quirky copier, and is able to coax a ream of forms out of the machine before papers start to jam. Perhaps another volunteer needs to quit stabbing the buttons hoping to intimidate the machine into working at all.

Review what volunteers have learned, and provide the tweaking—retraining—that's required to get everyone up to speed.

That's it: a trainer's job in a nutshell.

Trainers are teachers—teachers who work with adults, and who facilitate learning by using hands-on, active learning. That's a win for everyone, because skills and information are more easily learned and retained by volunteers when experienced in a practical, active way.

Plus, it's way more fun to teach!

As we consider how to design a training session, see how interaction and involvement are woven into the process. They're there for a reason.

FOUR
How to Design Training Sessions That Work

Nine strategic steps that let you deliver on-target training sessions—every time.

An effective training session starts long before volunteers walk into the room, fill out their nametags, and mingle by the coffeepot. The actual session is the part of the process people associate with training, but it's only the tip of the iceberg.

If you experience a training session that's informative, effective, and useful, you can bet the trainer began preparing for the session weeks before.

That's the decision you have to make first: Will you be disciplined in preparing for training sessions? If not, seek out someone who will, and delegate the training function of your ministry to that person. Training is too important to hope that when you wing it something good will come out of the experience.

> "Training requires thoughtful preparation."

Training requires thoughtful preparation. There's no shortcut.

Assuming you believe that training is worthy of your best effort, go through the following nine-step process to create on-target sessions that accomplish your goals.

Step 1: Determine the Need
What do people want and need to know? This is the step skipped by the hospital that was providing elaborate—and

largely meaningless—training to expectant mothers.

Some experts call it "gap analysis": identifying the space between the existing experience and knowledge of your volunteers, and what experience and knowledge they'll need to accomplish a task.

It's that gap between what they've got and what they'll need that training seeks to fill—so you'd better do a good job identifying the gap. Providing training for the wrong experiences and knowledge is useless.

Consider the experiences of a friend of ours named Brian . . .

Brian was determined to make his school basketball team after failing to make the squad the previous year. "I was the last guy cut," Brian remembers. "It about crushed me."

So Brian attended basketball camps and spent afternoons at city courts where he sharpened his skills in game after game of pick-up ball.

"I'd always been a timid player," Brian says, "afraid to get under the hoop and mix it up. But if you're not willing to throw a few elbows you got eaten alive out on the public courts—especially the ones where the really good street players hung out. Nobody called fouls out there; it was a matter of pride. You either intimidated the other players or you died."

> **"Brian watched—and learned."**

Brian watched—and learned. He mimicked better players and learned how to shave half-steps while driving to the basket. He practiced moves that eventually had him winning instead of watching, taking high-fives from players he respected.

Brian went from timid to intimidating. "I learned to take it to the bucket," he says. "Get in my way and you were going down. I could usually get around you, over you, under you—something. But if I couldn't—well, I went through you."

So Brian felt strong when he tried out for the varsity team his junior year.

"I put on a show for them right off the start," he says. "Once I had the ball I angled and cut my way to the basket.

Every time. I smoked the defense during our first scrimmage. Scored 28 points."

Brian went home sure he had impressed the coaches. And he had—they cut him from the tryouts the next day.

Stunned, Brian asked the head coach what had happened. He pointed out that he wasn't the player he'd once been, timid and shy. Now he was a scorer—and he'd proved it.

That's when the coach gave Brian the news: Brian hadn't been cut from the squad the previous year because he lacked the ability to score, or because he'd been weak on hitting the boards and bringing down rebounds. He'd been cut because the coach didn't think he was a team player.

And if anything, Brian was even worse now. He didn't pass, he didn't run plays, he just hot-dogged the ball and left the rest of the team standing around.

Brian had trained hard to improve—but in the wrong skill.

"I never made the team until my senior year," Brian says. "But I was high man on assists that year."

Ouch. Brian had done a poor job with "gap analysis."

Do your needs analysis carefully. Fixing the wrong thing doesn't move volunteers ahead; it leaves them further behind.

And it's important you not confuse activity with accomplishment when it comes to training. Holding training sessions is only useful if there are appropriate outcomes (ones that help fill the gap) that can be demonstrated by the

> "Ask volunteers what they need to know."

volunteers. Do they know how to operate the photocopy machine after your training session? That's actually easy to determine: Have them show you how to do it.

Did they truly learn? Also easy: Call them back in a week and ask them to demonstrate their retained skills.

Volunteers themselves may help you with needs analysis. Ask volunteers to tell you what they need to know. Ask their supervisors what they need to know. You may get a glimmer of what's needed when you interview or survey the people served by your volunteers. If Jack thinks he's doing a great job delivering Christian education and his supervisor agrees, but children aren't learning anything, there's a gap—and a need for training!

When thinking about training, start by determining what the volunteers need to be doing differently as a result of the training. Is the need they're experiencing one that can be met through more information? through using a new skill? through a shift in attitude?

How you understand the need sets the course of the entire training session.

Step 2: Establish Objectives

Okay, let's be realistic: A one- or two-hour training session isn't going to completely revolutionize how Jack teaches in the fourth-grade class. One session isn't going to somehow toggle on Jack's effectiveness switch so kids start learning, especially if you're going to present the training to the entire Sunday school teaching staff and can't focus solely on Jack.

But you can do this: Write clear objectives you think you can achieve given the number of learners, the various settings in which they deliver Christian education, and the amount of time you have for the session.

"Narrow down what you're trying to accomplish."

Narrow down what you're trying to accomplish. Instead of "figure out how to have every teacher become effective in engaging children and doubling students' learning" (lofty, but not probable), zero in on one skill classroom teachers could use to improve their teaching. Classroom management techniques, perhaps, or skills related to using active-learning techniques.

Write behavioral objectives—what volunteers will be able to do at the end of the training session. It may have to be demonstrated through role plays (as in the case of Jack dealing with his students), but be certain that volunteers can do a show and tell with the new skill or information.

And be absolutely certain that possessing the new skill or information will help address the need you identified in step 1.

Step 3: Create the Evaluation Tool

Decide how you'll have volunteers prove they've "gotten it" at the end of the training session, and create that evaluation tool now. Be specific, and design it so it answers the question, "How will volunteers prove they've achieved the session's objectives?"

Seems backward, doesn't it? Why create the test before you've created the training session?

It's because the evaluation tool pinpoints your destination. It identifies where you want to end up at the end of the session when volunteers are walking out the door. It measures the outcomes you identified in step 2.

Step 4: Brainstorm the Training Session

Working alone or with colleagues, think about the evaluation tool you've identified. Write it out and tape it to the far end of a white board. Then, with a marker in hand, ask, "Given where the learners are now, what do they need to learn to let them pass this evaluation exercise?"

> "Arrange your outline in a logical order."

The answer to your question—the steps and skills—are the content of the training session. You've created your session outline.

Step 5: Dig in—It's Time to Write a Session

Arrange your outline in a logical order. Before you flesh it out, though, ask yourself the following questions. Your answers will help you shape *how* you deliver the content of the training session to your volunteers.

And be warned: This will take some time.

You're pausing to consider how to tailor the training session so it powerfully connects with your volunteers—all your volunteers.

Think of it this way: Pretty much anyone can wander onto a softball diamond. Anyone can walk to the pitcher's mound. Anyone can stand there, face the catcher crouching behind home plate, and throw a softball to the catcher. It's only 46 feet, so it's not terribly difficult.

You lob the ball, and it gets to the catcher—either in the air, on the bounce, or rolling along in the dirt. If you lower the definition of "pitching" far enough, anyone can do it.

But to sizzle that ball into the strike zone, blistering it into the catcher's mitt—that takes some effort. It requires practice and preparation. And it's the sort of pitch that gets fans up on their feet and cheering.

Don't just settle for lobbing training sessions at your volunteers. Do what's necessary to make each one spectacular, streaking straight across home plate.

> **"Without motivation, there's no lasting learning."**

It comes down to delivery—and your answers to these questions will help you find and hit the strike zone every time.

- **How will I present this session in such a way that volunteers care?**

Without motivation, there's no lasting learning—so always establish to a volunteer's satisfaction why a skill must be mastered or information learned. What problem of the volunteer's will it solve to enthusiastically embrace the work required to accomplish the outcomes set for this training?

- **How can I build on information volunteers already possess?**

Do you actually know what people already know? You can establish this by using a pretest at the beginning of the training session and then adjusting the session depending on what you discover.

Clearly, this is a risky maneuver. You may discover that half your volunteers could lead the session, and the other half have no clue about the topic. More likely you'll find that volunteers fall along a continuum stretching from incompetent to very competent.

For instance, our Sunday school teacher friend, Jack, probably already knows something about classroom discipline. What he knows may be wrong, or it may be right, but he knows something.

If you're a beginning trainer, you may wish to skip pretests for a few sessions until your confidence builds. But then by all means use them—they'll let you know precisely how to meet the needs of your specific audience.

And—if you're lucky—you may find you have a valuable resource in the room that you can tap to make the training session even stronger.

> "If you're lucky you may find you have a valuable resource in the room."

That's what happened to a colleague of ours who, while he was a sophomore in Bible college 30 years ago, was asked to prepare a two-hour training session for a large multi-college retreat.

Here's his story . . .

The Accidental Professor

"I was leading a training session on hermeneutics, which is the science of interpretation—in this case the interpretation of Scripture. My audience included about a hundred college students, and I assumed that very few of them had even *heard* of hermeneutics. All they knew was that I would be sharing some principles that helped with Bible study.

"On a whim I took a quick poll. I asked how many had ever heard of hermeneutics, and only one hand was raised. When I saw whose hand it was, I nearly fainted.

"That hand was connected to a man I recognized as Lewis Foster, an academic who'd helped translate the New

International Version of the Bible. How could I lead a training session on Bible study with a Harvard Ph.D. sitting in the back of the room? A Harvard Ph.D. who was fluent in every ancient language except cave drawing? Who was I kidding?

"I figured the best thing I could do was have everyone turn their chairs around and I'd let Dr. Foster lead the training," our colleague admits. "I introduced him and made the offer, but he declined and moved to the front row. He encouraged me to continue and, knees shaking, that's what I did.

"Dr. Foster paid careful attention and frequently nodded in agreement as I spoke. My credibility with the audience shot up about four thousand percent every time his head went up and down," says our colleague.

"When there were questions, Dr. Foster let me answer first, and only added something if I'd completely gotten in over my head. When the session was over he shook my hand, congratulated me on a job well done, and walked out. That was an amazingly gracious guy."

Our colleague was fortunate that Dr. Foster chose to support rather than challenge him. Not every expert is so gracious.

If you find yourself in a situation where someone in your audience is truly better informed than you, and is intent on letting everyone know it, defuse the situation by reminding your audience that everyone will have time to speak later in the session. Most people take the hint.

- **How can I address various learning styles during the training?**

There have been several attempts to categorize learning styles, and each of them agrees on this point: Talking at people isn't the way to go.

There are people who learn best by seeing a demonstration, or who learn best by diving in and trying things themselves. There are logical thinkers and people who learn best when they're interacting with others. Still other people learn best through introspection . . . or through music . . . or through experiencing nature.

How can you possibly present all of the information in each of those styles?

You can't . . . but you can make sure there's something for everyone during the training session.

If you're helping Sunday school teachers learn how to handle classroom discipline, include these elements . . .

• Have volunteers tell stories about situations that have arisen. This will snag your verbal and linguistic learners.

• Ask visual learners to design a classroom setting that would minimize disruptions. Where would the teacher be? the students? What furniture would or wouldn't be in the room?

> "Make sure there's something for everyone during the training session."

• Ask musically inclined people to suggest a theme song for the chaotic classroom. What popular song (or classic song) sums up what it's like?

• Recruit kinesthetic learners to act out a skit about a typical classroom discipline challenge.

• Suggest that logical learners brainstorm ideas about what Sunday school teachers can do to overcome the discipline challenges.

• Issue this challenge to the naturalists in your audience: What lessons are there in nature about how to deal with disruptions from children (and no, teachers can't eat their young!)?

• Give interpersonal learners the chance to work together to plan an event where people could find answers around the challenge of classroom discipline. Who would attend? What would happen?

• For intrapersonal learners, ask them to describe how they feel when children sabotage their lessons.

Will all these fit in a single training session? It will help if you have a breakout session that allows people to choose between several of the activities so they can plug in where they're most comfortable. And even if you can't accommodate every learning style, the more you can use, the more people in your audience will think you're speaking directly to them.

• **How can I make this session interactive?**

It's less difficult than you might imagine. Including peer-to-peer discussion in small groups or pair-shares is a great place to start.

Consider breaking out small groups to each tackle a piece of a carefully identified problem, with each group then coming back with its piece of the jigsaw puzzle. This is a great way not only to be interactive, but to build ownership of the solution that eventually emerges.

Look for places to effectively use activities, exercises, discussions of case studies, team building or team work, brainstorming—they're all ways to include interactive learning.

Picture the person who'll attend who's most likely to be thinking of something else. Maybe it's Jerry, who always appears to be taking notes, but you know he is actually filling out work-related expense reports. Or Samantha, who drums her fingers and fidgets if she's forced to sit still for more than ten minutes.

Here's your goal: Design a training session that Samantha can tolerate and that will have Jerry checking his watch when the session ends, wondering where the time went.

• **How can I intentionally encourage volunteers in the context of this training session?**

What will you say or do that affirms volunteers in their service and faithfulness? Saying "thanks for coming" is a good start, but you'll have more opportunity as the training session unfolds. Add to this list . . .

> • Know the names of volunteers when they arrive. Greet them by name—before they fill out nametags.

- Know what each volunteer does in ministry so you can ask specific questions and keep the training relevant.

- Affirm individuals for their contributions.

- Pray for individuals, asking God to bless them.

Once volunteers are serving in a ministry role, occasional training sessions may be the only face-to-face time you have with some volunteers. Don't miss the chance to remind them that what they do is ministry, and that their ministry is appreciated.

> "Affirm individuals for their contributions."

- **How can I encourage volunteers to grow in their relationship with Jesus in the context of this training session?**

Remember one of the core values of volunteer leadership: One outcome of participating as a volunteer needs to be growth in the volunteer's relationship with Jesus.

Never lose sight of this value! Let it slip from view and you're simply recruiting people to do jobs. You're no longer involving them in significant ministry that changes lives—including the volunteer's own life.

Ways you can encourage relational growth with Jesus at a training session include . . .

- Praying with the volunteers.

- Asking volunteers what impact their volunteer experience is having on their relationship with Jesus. Let them tell you!

- Sharing a devotion together, perhaps one prepared by one of the volunteers.

What else could you do? With your content outline and your answers to the questions listed above, you're ready to finish creating the training session. Keep in mind the limitations you face regarding time and space (no sense planning to illustrate teamwork by playing a full-court volleyball game if you'll meet in a classroom), and go to it. Craft a workshop that covers the material and integrates the insights you gained by thinking about how you'll shape the delivery of your training session.

Step 6: Develop a Great Opening

How you launch into your training session is very important. It's when you reel in your volunteers and get them focused and concentrating, or it's the precise moment you lose them—maybe for the entire session.

Because of that, be very intentional about how you begin your session.

A word of caution: Be wary of humor. If your joke falls flat, or your humor somehow offends a volunteer, you're sunk.

A stronger opening will be some way to illustrate the point that the subject matter you'll cover together will solve a problem experienced in the volunteers' lives. Establish that the training is relevant and there's a benefit, and you're home free.

"Be wary of humor."

Step 7: Decide on an Icebreaker to Use in Your Session

Even if you suspect all your volunteers know each other, icebreakers are a good idea at the beginning of your session. Why? Because they do three important things:

- They focus attention. Your volunteers are tired, busy, and at least partially wishing they could be doing other things. When you get them actively involved you force volunteers to be present in the moment.

- They're fun. Ask most volunteers what they expect to experience at a training session and you'll wait a long time before you hear "fun." That's because the expectation is that training is boring. Not true! Start your session out on the right foot by exceeding volunteers' expectations immediately with a few minutes of good, clean fun!

- And, if the volunteers truly hate icebreakers, you unite them against a common enemy: you! Perhaps this is a bit overstated, but if you're enthusiastically asking volunteers to do something that stretches them past their comfort level, they'll all be on the same page. You can build from there by acknowledging their willingness to try new things, and promising you'll never again ask each person to sing a verse of his or her favorite show tune.

Four Fool-Proof, Easy-Prep, No-Fail Icebreakers

Enjoy!

Find the Fib

Ask each volunteer to tell three stories about his or her life that highlight something nobody at the meeting knows—except one of the stories is a fib.

This is easier for new people whose history is largely unknown, but everyone has something from their childhood that isn't generally known. A first job, an unusual skill, an odd experience while on vacation; they're all grist for the mill.

Have volunteers form groups of three or four and take turns sharing stories. Then, after a volunteer talks, ask the other group members to vote on which story was a fib. Following the vote, let the storyteller reveal the truth.

Guess the Pet

This is a simple icebreaker that uses nametags. In addition to writing his or her name, ask each volunteer to also write the name of a childhood pet. After all the volunteers have arrived, form volunteers into groups of four and try to guess what sort of animal the pet was.

This icebreaker finally rewards the person who once named a pet boa constrictor "Fluffy."

Decipher the Code

Another nametag icebreaker. In addition to writing his or her name, ask each volunteer to also write a number that has significance in his or her life.

For instance, if a woman was married on May 23, 1987, the number written would be 52387. If a man's childhood home was 1011 Pennway Lane, the number might be 1011. After all the volunteers have arrived, form volunteers into groups of four and try to decipher what the numbers mean by asking yes and no questions.

Brush with Greatness

Amazingly fun—but it takes a bit of explaining.

The goal is to have each volunteer consider some connection he or she has to someone great (or at least famous) and to share it. The vaguer the connection, the better.

For instance, "I used to babysit for George Clooney" is strong, but "My uncle was once knocked out by a stray golf ball hit by President Ford" is stronger. You'll be amazed at the life some of your volunteers have led.

Step 8: Practice

Never let the time you stand up in front of a group of volunteers be the first time you've run completely through a training session. Practice walking through the session at least twice to test the timing of the activities and to be sure your notes are clear to you.

Some ministry leaders actually do the entire training session with peers to get their feedback.

Also, this is a good time to think about how you'll set up the location where you'll be doing the training session. Do you need audio or visual equipment? Will you need to be able to control the lighting? Do the chairs need to be set up in any particular configuration or removed altogether? Are there props for you to gather, or people who will be working with you in presenting the material? snacks or notepads and pens to have available? nametags to fill out before volunteers arrive?

Logistics are part of the practice session. Be sure you know what you'll need, and have it ready to go before the eleventh hour. The eleventh hour is reserved for prayer and whatever crisis comes up to throw you off track.

Step 9: Ask for and Value Feedback

Build two feedback loops into your training sessions. The first is already in place: the ability or inability of the volunteers to do what was set as an objective. If your training was effective, it should have had an impact on their abilities to meet the objective.

But use another feedback loop, too: surveys from volunteers who have gone through the training session.

A sample training session evaluation begins on page 101. Adapt it to suit your situation, but please note that unless you include open-ended questions to prompt a candid evaluation, you won't learn much from surveys. If you train enough volunteers at a time to make it practical for volunteers to believe their responses can be anonymous, remove the opportunity for volunteers to report their names. If you have ten or fewer volunteers in a session, they probably doubt they can stay anonymous anyway, so ask for names.

Those nine steps will guide you through designing on-target training sessions, but there are still things you could profit from knowing. Among them are the two dozen tips for trainers we've gathered from top-notch trainers from around the country and included in the next chapter.

Read through the list with a highlighter in hand. Mark those nuggets that you know would improve your training sessions or your skills as a trainer.

How to Get Volunteers to Actually Show Up for Training Sessions

Frank was busy. Things came up for Sarah. Jeff was unexpectedly called out of town on a job-related trip. Terri was on vacation. Joni's kids got sick. The in-laws dropped by unannounced for a visit at Mike's house. Hannah forgot. Dirk's dog died.

Host training sessions long enough and you'll be convinced there's no such thing as a new excuse—until you hear one. And you will hear one. It's frustrating to prepare training sessions and have people who have agreed to come—and who need the training—not show up.

Here are six things you can do to prompt higher attendance . . .

1. Realize it's true: Sometimes things *do* come up.

Very few of us have perfect attendance for anything. Be graceful when volunteers encounter illnesses, broken water heaters, emergency dental visits, and other schedule-changing events.

2. Be sure training is an up-front expectation.

Outline what's expected in terms of training in the job description. Mention it at meetings. Talk about it in newsletters. And always connect training with the benefits that come from it.

3. Provide lots of advance notice.

Schedule your meetings well in advance, and if possible make them consistent. It's easier to clear a spot on the calendar if it's predictable, such as the last Sunday evening of each month.

4. Remove obstacles.

Provide child care. Include a meal if the session approaches meal time. Be as adaptable and accommodating as possible.

5. Consider alternate training methods.

You probably can't get all your volunteers to set aside a full day for training. It just doesn't happen any more. If attendance for training events is slipping, perhaps you stop asking "When should we meet?" and start asking, "How would you like to receive training?"

Options include:

Mentoring—which can be arranged at the convenience of the mentor and mentoree.

On-line training—(as through Group's Church Volunteer Central) that lets volunteers log on at their convenience.

Independent study opportunities—which could include video courses, workbooks, books to read and review, and audio tapes.

Bite-size training—such as e-mails that address just one teaching skill, an answering machine with a brief training tip that volunteers can call at any hour, or five-minute meetings on Sunday mornings before a worship service or between services.

Observation/coaching—which involves a trainer watching a volunteer in action and then giving specific feedback to the volunteer.

If a volunteer opts for non-traditional training, it will increase the amount of work you—or someone on your task force or board—will have to do. But the result is better trained volunteers.

6. Ask volunteers to write one-year training plans.

Remember: Including people in a process builds buy-in to the process. Let volunteers know what training is available, what level of training is appropriate for their role, and ask them what sessions they wish to take. Hold volunteers accountable with regular check-ins.

FIVE
Two Dozen Tips for Trainers

Training is art as well as science. Here are things top-notch trainers have discovered to be true—you can put them to use in your own volunteer ministry training sessions today!

Training is a bit like cooking: It involves both science and art.

When you're trying for the perfect lasagna, you've got to master the science first. The temperature of the oven, the acidity of the tomato sauce, the thickness of the noodles; that's the science. It's unforgiving and non-negotiable. Mess up how long you leave the pan in the oven and you've either got lasagna soup or lasagna jerky. Neither is anything close to the perfect lasagna.

But master the science and now you can express your art. Exactly how much cheese do you add? And what kinds of cheese? Ah—that's when you delight people lucky enough to get a dinner invitation to your house. And when you start to develop the secret of your own family recipe.

> "Training is a bit like cooking: It involves both science and art."

We hounded some excellent "cooks" to get their secrets for successful training sessions. Here are the tips they shared. Two dozen that you can serve up to make your perfect training session even better.

1. Multi-sensory learning lasts longer—so never settle for lecturing. Find ways to involve the senses, and wrap stories into your training. Emotional content also touches people in significant ways. You'll notice you can remember the joke the pastor shared as a sermon introduction far longer than you can remember the sermon itself. Take advantage of the power of story.

2. Learning is most successful when stress from environment, emotional factors, and external commitments are reduced. This is one reason that what happens in the first five minutes of your training session is so vitally important. If you can focus volunteers, convincing them to set aside their concerns for the duration of your training session, you'll see more learning happen.

Here's a technique that you can use if all else fails: Open the door into the hallway outside your room and invite all the concerns and worries being experienced by your volunteers to wait outside. Tell volunteers they can pick up their concerns after the training session is over—but for the duration those concerns will be waiting in the hall.

3. Past experience should be part of the present learning. Build on what people already know—how they already think and what they already understand—and you'll find people are quicker to accept what you say.

4. What you present first and last will be retained in a disproportionate degree. It's the way we tend to listen to each other: What's said first and last counts most. So start strong and sum up at the end; those two portions of your training are your best chance to make an impression.

5. Success reinforces learning. It's better to cover something limited and do it so volunteers experience success than to attempt to cover more and fail. Break skill training into bite-size pieces. Dumping a ton of information on volunteers just buries them.

energy you invest will communicate the importance of training and jazz up the experience without spending a fortune to take your team to Hawaii for a beachfront training session.

14. Integrate mentoring into your training process. If a volunteer serves as a teacher, arrange for regular visits from a master teacher who'll observe and provide help reaching the next level. If a volunteer makes hospital visits, ask the hospital chaplain to team up with your volunteer for a visit or two, then talk with your volunteer about how to be even more effective. Training doesn't have to be a separate event hosted quarterly in a special room at church.

15. Build variety into your training. When you're communicating content, use as many media and methods as you're comfortable using. Keep in mind that when people hear information, they retain little of it. When they roll up their sleeves and immediately use that information, it becomes part of who they are.

Use technology that the church already owns. Find out what it takes to plug into the PowerPoint dock, and use the video projector to show film clips.

16. It's okay to repeat yourself. If you do a session on emergency evacuation procedures, consider following up your formal training with a fire drill followed by a refresher course followed by another fire drill. Over the course of a few months the information will sink deep into what your volunteers know—and what they've practiced doing. And a practice evacuation costs nothing.

17. Consider "certifying" some positions. There's nothing wrong with having "usher certification" that demonstrates that the certified usher has been through a training course, been mentored by a certified usher, and has passed a ten-question exam that includes the questions an usher is most likely to be asked.

The cost of developing a certification program? Almost nothing—just the training, the testing, and a certificate designed on your computer.

18. Build feedback loops into your training. If training sessions are characteristically you talking and everyone else listening, you may be surprised how little training is actually taking place.

The goal of training is for volunteers to retain and use information, not just to be exposed to it. Remember that talking isn't necessarily teaching, and listening isn't necessarily learning.

19. Let volunteers apply new knowledge immediately. There's a half-life on learning. Unless volunteers use it fairly quickly, it tends to slip away because it has not been applied. Be intentional about providing opportunities to apply learning quickly!

Best is to actually put new knowledge to use, but a great deal will be retained even if the best you can offer is simulation or practice sessions. Anything that moves theory down to practical application is a plus!

20. Make emotional connections. Use stories as well as statistics. If you fire off a long string of numbers you'll see eyes glaze over—fast. Mix it up, and be sure that even statistics are presented in such a way that there's an emotional response on the part of your training audience. You're looking to make an emotional connection, to build on the material being presented, and to add to other, existing interests of your audience.

21. Keep things interesting. Volunteers who have given up a Saturday for a training session will forgive almost anything except boredom. You forgot to bring a snack—no problem, everyone will live. You ran ten minutes overtime—well, you'll do better next time.

But if you're boring, you're dead. Beat boredom by being interactive; use group projects and discussions. Design your session so more than one learning style is tapped.

And personalize the training to keep it relevant. Volunteers are much more interested when you're helping them solve an immediate problem than when you're passing on information they don't see an immediate need to have.

Find a need and design training to meet it!

> "Beat boredom by being interactive."

22. Training isn't always the solution. If you have a volunteer who seems unable to be successful in a role after training, coaching, and several second chances, it's possible that volunteer will never be successful. The task may be beyond the volunteer's ability. You may have misunderstood the volunteer's abilities, skills, or passions for ministry. Move the volunteer to a new role and start over. Sometimes it's wise to cut your losses.

23. Bring snacks. Always. There's nothing like a plate of homemade chocolate chip cookies to win a training group over.

24. Use experts. A sad fact: Everyone knows you, so you must not know much. But if you find someone in a neighboring church who has the same knowledge you have, that person is an expert!

Dig for resource people willing to provide training at no (or low) cost. They're out there. A professional teacher in your church or a neighboring church can speak to classroom discipline. A counselor can share training about conflict resolution or listening. Who has expertise in your circle of acquaintances? You can often find a true expert at a local college, or involved in a local church, and get the benefit of that person's expertise for the cost of mileage reimbursement and a thank-you gift.

A caution: Knowing something doesn't mean you know how to teach it. You'll need to work with presenters to make sure they design training that's on target.

And a bonus tip:

25. Keep track. What gets measured gets reported, and what gets reported is usually what matters. Know who comes to training events and who doesn't—and keep track of attendance. If attendance is part of the volunteer's job description, immediately follow up with no-shows to find out why they missed and to arrange make-up training.

There's nothing like watching a session on video to convince a no-show that it would have been more fun to be there in person.

The cost of recording the training session? A call to borrow a video camera, asking a teenager to do the taping, and a videotape.

SIX
Training Approaches for Small Churches—and Busy People

How do you keep training sessions from overwhelming your schedule? Here are three ways to keep training in check—but still effective.

Some trainers estimate that preparing a one-hour training session can take up to 10 hours. When you consider how much research is required to do a needs analysis and then work through designing a session, that estimate doesn't seem far-fetched. In fact, it may be conservative.

So here you are, the lone person responsible for your church's volunteer ministry. Where are you going to find time to create and lead training for the dozen different volunteer jobs you have to fill?

And another question: Why should you create a formal youth leader training program when you only need to recruit, place, and train one youth volunteer? It doesn't make sense!

> "There is never a reason for setting a volunteer up for failure."

Except it does make sense.

What doesn't make sense is letting a volunteer enter a job for which he or she isn't prepared, and then letting the volunteer fail for lack of knowledge or skills. Especially when we know we could come alongside the volunteer and help that person flourish in the ministry role.

Stand firm on this point: There is never a reason for setting a volunteer up for failure. Never. If a ministry isn't ready to receive a volunteer, or a volunteer isn't ready to take on the role, don't force it. The result will be disappointment and failure all the way around.

Which means what? That you have to provide all the training?

Not necessarily.

How Specialized Does Your Training Program Need to Be?

You've got volunteers doing everything from accounting to lawn care. How much specific task-related training is worth providing?

Asking these questions will help you make that determination . . .

- Are there volunteers serving in roles that require continuing education units, licensing, or certification by the government? If so, what responsibility does the church feel for helping volunteers maintain their certification? any? all? You probably can't provide the actual training; the decision you need to make is whether you'll pay for any or all of it since the church benefits from it.

- What are logical groupings of volunteers who need training? For instance, do you have fifteen educators who could use training, but just two puppeteers? If you have time to design just a few specialized training sessions, where will you get the "biggest bang for your buck"?

- What new skills and knowledge do volunteers need to master for your ministry to reach a goal that's already in place? For instance, if the church plans to open a day care center and to utilize volunteers in some roles, there are training considerations to address before the day care's doors open for business.

- What funding is available for training?

- Is there expertise your team has developed that can be organized into training that could be provided for other churches? And if so, would charging for that training generate money to support or expand your ministry?

- What incentives are in place to encourage volunteers to seek additional training? What obstacles are in place that interfere with training? You won't be a happy camper if you prepare training sessions and nobody comes.

Here's where you probably landed after answering those questions:

You want trained volunteers, and the benefits that come with training.

Some jobs seem to require very little training.

You don't have time to train everyone.

You aren't sure what to do.

Join Donna

Welcome to the club. That's precisely where Donna found herself when she assumed the role of Director of Volunteers for her church of two hundred.

"We had most of the programs operating that a church of a thousand has," she says, "which meant we were really stretched on covering the jobs."

Donna did what she could, but some jobs went unfilled because there wasn't anyone in the church who was appropriately gifted to fill them. In other cases there were people serving, but only one or two per job category.

> "How could I possibly justify writing a training session for Matt?"

"I found myself wondering how I could possibly justify writing a training session for Matt, who was responsible for stacking chairs in our worship center after Sunday morning worship celebrations. He put the chairs on a rack and rolled the rack into a closet. What was I supposed to train him to do?"

Here's the thing: With the church sitting at an attendance of 200, Matt didn't really need a formal one-hour training session. Doing a five-minute demonstration handled it. But if the church grew to a thousand, and the ten rows of chairs multiplied into a sea of chairs, what then?

Matt would need help. How should he go about recruiting volunteers? scheduling them? supervising them?

Matt would probably need to lock up the building because he and his crew would take longer to accomplish the task. What responsibilities came with having a key to the worship center?

Matt would need to do periodic evaluations of his volunteers. How could he do that without them having a job description? And him having one as well?

Because the church was still small, Donna had the luxury of not creating a formal training session. She still needed to create a job description, provide an orientation, and train Matt to do the task, and for the moment that was enough.

But if the church grew and Matt's role changed, formal training would be needed. And the lack of it would eventually become obvious. Failing to provide in-depth training is like burying a land mine; sooner or later it will be triggered.

Because of demands on her time, Donna has found three innovative ways to provide training—including a technique she used to train Matt.

Decide if these techniques will work for you, too . . .

1. Training Sheila

"A decision to expand our Sunday morning program to include a children's church service threw us for a loop," says Donna. "None of our children's ministry team had ever actually led worship for elementary students."

So Donna called the children's worship team leader at a nearby, larger church. And after identifying who would be leading the new ministry, that person attended a month of services at the other church. "They were incredibly helpful," says Donna. "Sheila got training from their staff, and learned what worked and didn't work for them. It shortened our learning curve dramatically. Our program got up and running far quicker because of what Sheila learned."

Which raises the question: Is your church the best place to get the training your people need? Be open to calling other churches—and being called by other churches in turn. What churches in your community might be willing to help you?

> "Donna called the children's worship leader at a larger church."

Donna still needed to create job descriptions, but she was able to get some from the other church to adapt. And again—if your church is part of Group's Church Volunteer Central there's a wealth of job descriptions available for your review at www.churchvolunteercentral.com.

Donna will also need to eventually create (or have Sheila create) training sessions for additional children's church staff who come into the program, but that can wait until everyone catches their breath.

2. Training Bruce

Donna's church building sat on a corner one block away from a university campus, which meant that you might expect the congregation to have a vibrant outreach to college students.

You'd be wrong.

"Some of our members were students, but given that dorms housing more than two thousand students sat within three blocks, we weren't being very effective reaching them."

The pastor decided to launch a visitation program in the dorms. "We looked around the congregation and found we had a retired military recruiter who was worshiping with us.

He knew all the people who ran the dorms, he was used to knocking on doors, and he was passionate about his faith. Perfect, right?"

Perfect, except he didn't want the job.

"He told us he'd retired from knocking on doors. He had zero interest in doing it again, even for the church."

So Donna shifted her request. Instead of actually going on visits, would the man be willing to pass on what he knew to someone else? Would he become a trainer?

> "Perfect, except he didn't want the job."

After some deliberation, the ex-recruiter agreed, and Donna found Bruce, who was willing to go to the dorms and to build a team to go with him, but who lacked experience connecting with college students and establishing relationships.

The result was a successful program. And once it was up and running the ex-recruiter decided to take an active role after all.

Donna arranged for Bruce to receive the training he needed, but not from her. And if you're willing to isolate training into modules, you may find you don't need to do all the training, either.

Bruce needed two sorts of training: how to share his faith, and how to be comfortable inviting students to participate in a program. Donna knew how to deliver the first sort of training, but not the second. That's where the ex-recruiter came in.

In your congregation are there teachers and principals available who aren't interested in teaching a class—but they'd train teachers? Are there professional salesmen who would be willing to train your ushers how to make eye contact, shake hands, and engage people? Are there counselors who can teach your small group leaders how to actively listen? The possibilities are almost endless.

3. Training Matt

Back to the man with a chair rack and a mission . . .

Donna recognized the need for Matt to have some help, so

she encouraged him to recruit a few chair stackers who could give him a hand, learn the ropes, and then cover for him when he happened to be out of town.

Donna developed a job description, which one of the stackers—the vice-president of a multi-million dollar insurance company whose corporate office was in town—was delighted to receive. He had it framed and hung it in his office as a reminder that service, not status, was the highest calling.

And the formal training session? Donna never developed it.

"I couldn't find a skill gap," Donna reports. "This is a narrow enough task that we can cover it with OTJ—on the job training. Matt can explain the entire procedure to his helpers in about five minutes, so I'm letting orientation take care of the training."

> "Where can you use OTJ training in your volunteer ministry?"

At last look the system is doing fine—chairs get stacked and put away, and nobody has needed a training session to do it.

Where can you use OTJ training in your volunteer ministry? At what point do you need to move past it and structure formal training?

SEVEN
Track Your Training

Training isn't cheap, so get the biggest bang for your buck by tracking your volunteers' training history—and planning ahead.

You're ready to do it: Make sure every volunteer is trained. You're willing to invest time, energy, and even—perhaps—budget on creating effective training sessions. You've got a dozen or two dozen or two *dozen* dozen volunteers moving through your training sessions.

It's beginning to feel like you're running a university, not a volunteer program.

But can you remember which volunteer has taken which seminar, session, or class? Do you know if you have enough CPR-trained volunteers whose certification is current? Are there enough volunteers who've taken the driver safety course that your insurance agency insists on for adults who transport special needs kids? Do you know which training sessions are most useful for someone who's volunteering in Christian education as opposed to, say, the Christmas pageant?

Different programs in your church have different training needs. Volunteers themselves have different training needs depending on the demands of their volunteer roles or their own skill levels. Or new training may be required because somewhere along the way the requirements for being a volunteer receptionist changed, and only those with computer skills need apply.

You need to track the training you provide—on several levels.

- **You need to know which volunteers have completed specific sessions.**

If completion of specific sessions is a prerequisite for serving in certain roles (for example, "Nursery volunteers must complete the nursery orientation and the infant CPR class"), then you'd better be able to know who's done what, and when. And don't count on being able to remember.

Try this: Recite which courses you took during your last semester of high school. Now list the eight people who sat closest to you in homeroom.

Right—we didn't think you could do it. Few people can. And if you'll put a system in place to track your volunteers' ongoing participation in training, you won't need to remember. You can use those brain cells for more important things, like figuring out where you stashed your yearbook so you can look up the answers to those questions we asked you.

- **You need to know which training sessions have proven to be most helpful to your volunteers.**

If your most long-term nursery volunteers all credit Janice's training about how babies learn as their motivation for sticking with the program, that's something you want to know. And it's probably a reason you'll want every nursery volunteer exposed to Janice's training program.

> **"Training has an impact."**

Training has an impact, and it's not only measurable by determining whether the objective was obtained. It's also measurable longitudinally, by seeing how it impacts long-term behavior and attitudes. If you have a tracking system in place you can see trends develop that will allow you to proactively place people in training sessions.

Create Tracking Systems

At minimum, create a folder for each volunteer to update which training sessions have been completed, and when. What you place in folders depends in part on where you'll keep them.

If you're planning to include the notes taken during volunteers' placement interviews and the results of background checks, you must treat folders as confidential, keep them in a locked cabinet, and monitor who has access to the keys. Your volunteers were assured of appropriate confidentiality when they were interviewed; you must maintain it.

If you're simply tracking sessions taken and ongoing notes about sessions that might be appropriate, you're probably safe having the information easily accessible. But check with legal counsel first; if all records you maintain are considered personnel files, take appropriate precautions.

And the same holds true if you use computer spreadsheets to track sessions.

How to track training your volunteers have completed

A sample Continuing Education Sheet is available for your adaptation and use on page 103. Create a sheet for each of your volunteers.

The title of the sheet is strategic; most educators are familiar with the term "continuing education," and it sets an expectation that volunteers will continue to grow in their knowledge and skills.

Plus, the term is broader than just the training sessions you offer at your church. As you'll see in the next section, continuing education can come from many sources—and it's good for you to note any that volunteers bring to your attention.

If you have a medical doctor who attends a neurology conference and spends two days learning about how children learn, do you think a distilled version of that information will be of value to your Sunday school teachers? Absolutely! Indicate the doctor's training event on her sheet; you may want to tap her expertise later to create a training session.

Of course, none of your volunteers are accustomed to reporting what happens at work when they go to church. Few of your staff will think to tell you that they were out of town for a convention that included significant training.

That's why you'll have to ask.

During the meeting when you introduce the Continuing

Education Sheet, suggest examples of how work training might apply to your church's programs and volunteers.

Some possibilities might be . . .

A police officer who receives training on child safety and can then provide insight into how your children's ministry department might be better equipped to protect children in its care,

An accountant whose continuing education class includes up-to-date information about what volunteers can and can't deduct as charitable donations when it comes to serving at the church,

A buyer for a craft store who is given a close-up look at new craft materials coming out in the next year, and can then suggest decorating items to the vacation Bible school director.

Ask your volunteers what they know and what they're learning that might be helpful to other volunteers. Add a quick comment at staff meetings that you'd like to hear about any training your volunteers have received—any training at all. You may choose to not follow up on some items (the hunter who passed his expert marksman course probably won't be able to turn it into a training session), but you'll know the expertise is available.

You can serve as the center of that information web, but only if you recall what you've been told . . . which brings you back to filling out your volunteers' continuing education sheets and updating them regularly.

How to track which training sessions are most useful

This is a three-step process:

1. Document what you've done.

You first need to document what training has been offered through your volunteer ministry and the content of each session. Without a record of that information, you'll never be able to determine which of those sessions was most valuable.

If you aren't already capturing notes from each training session, start at once. If possible, videotape or audiotape each session, too. This allows you to have a library of "instant" training sessions for volunteers who enter a ministry and need to get up to speed. It also allows you to know, in two years, what happened in that training session everyone says changed their lives.

Remember how you couldn't recall which training session every volunteer took? You won't remember the content of each training session, either—even the ones you led.

Capture the content and keep it on file.

2. Create a catalog.

Create a catalog of training sessions you offer, and keep it current. Include descriptions of the sessions and what each session's objectives are—why a volunteer would want to attend. Also indicate who leads the session.

If you feel there's a need to offer the session regularly (once per year, once per semester, or whatever), go ahead and schedule it on the church calendar now. Though orientation sessions are often "on demand" sessions, given when the volunteer first signs on, many training sessions can be taken after a volunteer is in place.

You'll need the catalog when you implement the third step in the evaluation process—asking current volunteers to indicate which training sessions were especially helpful to them.

3. Ask for feedback.

Give each volunteer a sheet listing the training sessions he or she has attended, a copy of the catalog, and a copy of the Best Ever Sheet. A sample copy of a Best Ever Sheet is on page 104, and you're welcome to use and adapt it.

> "Look for trends by ministry area and by success of the volunteers."

The catalog will serve as a memory-jogger for volunteers. It's unlikely volunteers will remember the names of sessions they attended eight months earlier, but they'll probably recall the names of the trainers and the course objectives that were achieved.

Ask volunteers to complete the Best Ever Sheet and turn it in to you. As you collect a number of Best Ever Sheets, look for trends by ministry area and by success of the volunteers.

If your top-performing small group leaders all cite a few training sessions as beneficial, be sure that every small group leader goes through those sessions.

To be sure, there are variables when it comes to training sessions. The person presenting can play a huge role in making a session enjoyable and communicating the content effectively.

The relevance of the material may change depending on what's happening in the church or culture.

And the timing of the session can play a role, too. A session on "how to lead small groups of children" will be far more timely the week before vacation Bible school than during Christmas break. Volunteers who attend will be able to use the learning almost immediately in the summer, and in the winter they'll be distracted by the holiday.

But trends will emerge—and only by tracking them can the big picture of what you should put in place as standard training emerge. Your goal is in several years to determine a baseline of training sessions every volunteer should go through, and a second tier of training for each ministry group.

And may we encourage you to eventually add training sessions that are more for your volunteers than their roles? For instance, most volunteers are busy people. They might appreciate a training session on how to maintain life balance, or a session on time management—anything that helps reduce stress.

Adding a few "personal fulfillment" sessions as elective training will make your volunteer ministry a friendlier place to serve.

Sources for Training and Trainers

One way to add variety to training sessions is to make sure it's not always you leading them. Several sources of alternate training sources have been mentioned already, but for your convenience here's an expanded list. How many of these sources have you tapped?

Community experts

Contact the United Way, fraternal groups, or college instructors who teach courses in areas that are of interest. Not all will have a ready list of experts who are eager to come lead training, but some will. And for the cost of mileage and a warm handshake you can have real experts provide input.

Do a thorough job briefing outside speakers about your group and what to expect. Be clear about your values and the outcomes you want the training to provide. Work with the experts to reach a clear understanding of what they'll cover. And seek permission to record their presentation before the training event itself. Some experts may be uncomfortable granting permission.

"You have some experts at your church."

Inside experts

You have some experts at your church, you know.

Be on the lookout for training that your volunteers experience in their professional lives that could easily translate to their volunteer roles—or someone else's volunteer roles. Your doctor who learned about brain research and learning might sing in the choir, but the expertise is relevant to your Christian education department. If the doctor is willing, ask her to work with you to create and lead a training session with your children's workers.

Seminars

Take advantage of training offered in your area by Christian publishers or Christian organizations.

One such seminar for children's ministry is the Children's Ministry Magazine Live Workshop (offered by Group Publishing annually). The inexpensive pricing on most half-day or one-day seminars makes it possible for you to take your entire staff.

Similar touring seminars are available for other groups of volunteers in your church.

Training with other churches

If your training session is skill-based rather than centered on knowledge specific to your church, invite other churches to attend. "How to relate to youth" is going to be valuable to youth workers of all denominations, and it will cost you very little more to present the training to a room of thirty people instead of a room of ten.

A bonus: Ask for the same courtesy in return, and take advantage of training provided by other churches.

Books and articles

It's very possible you'll never see the items again, so don't circulate anything you feel you can't live without. But publications that address relevant issues can be shared among those volunteers who could benefit from them. The secret is to attach an interactive routing slip and to make it easy for volunteers to pass along the publications.

If volunteers have a box or a mail slot in the church office, this is fairly simple. If not, as a team work together to create a system for exchanging items in a timely fashion.

If you discover that many of the helpful articles are from one or two magazines, contact the publisher and ask for a group discount subscription. Then you can distribute the entire magazine to appropriate volunteers.

An interactive routing slip is on page 106 for you to adapt for your use.

When these articles or books return to you (think positively!), add them to a permanent library of source material. If they were worth circulating, they're worth keeping.

On the other hand, if you wouldn't keep the information, don't interrupt your volunteers' lives with a request they read it.

Show and Tell

If you or a colleague in the volunteer ministry attends a convention or seminar that's paid for by the church, set it as policy that the person who attends must present what was learned when the person returns. This policy keeps your attendee sharp and on the lookout for usable ideas while at the convention, not lying on the beach instead of attending sessions.

An easy way to position this is to ask for a show and tell session that describes three ideas volunteers can put to use immediately and three that should be considered long-term.

Give convention-goers a large tote to fill with materials from the convention vendors, too. Often there are great give-aways that can be used at the church. If the bag gets too cumbersome, it can be shipped to the church instead of being dragged on the plane.

> "Ask for a show and tell session."

And finally, give your convention-eers 20 or 30 dollars to buy audio tapes of sessions that were especially useful. Listening to a tape as you drive isn't the same as being there, but it's an affordable way to experience the workshop. And the tapes can become part of your permanent library.

Orientation and Training As a Retention Tool

Does it seem odd to think of your orientation and training as tools that keep volunteers active in your church? It actually makes perfect sense.

The effort you invest in creating outstanding orientation and training opportunities communicates to volunteers. It sends a signal.

It signals that someone—you—notices them and is concerned about their comfort and effectiveness. They know you're willing to go the second mile to see they have the skills and information they need.

It signals that you value them, and that they're part of a team.

It signals that they serve in a church and a ministry program where they're encouraged to grow in their own faith, their own skills, and their own relationship with Jesus.

And who wouldn't want to hang around a place like that?

Your efforts are sending a signal, all right. It's a signal of loving concern.

Thanks for what you're doing for and with your volunteers. Together you're accomplishing amazing things.

And here's good news: There are more amazing things for you ahead in the next volume of this Volunteer Leadership Series. You'll focus on volunteer encouragement, evaluation, and accountability—with a close look at recognizing volunteers, too.

Onward and upward!

Training Forms for Volunteers

Sample Volunteer Handbook Acknowledgment Form

Please complete this form and return it to the Director of Volunteer Ministries. Before you can be placed in a volunteer role, this form must be on file in the Volunteer Ministries' office.

Please read this handbook carefully. It contains the policies, procedures, philosophy, and expectations relating to volunteering at First Christian Church. When you've completed reviewing this handbook please complete and sign the following statement. Return it to _____, the Director of Volunteer Ministries.

A copy of this acknowledgement form appears at the back of this handbook for your records.

I, _____, acknowledge that I've received and read a copy of First Christian Church's Volunteer Handbook. The Handbook contains the policies, procedures, philosophy, and expectations relating to volunteering at First Christian Church.

I've familiarized myself, at least generally, with the contents of this handbook. My signature below acknowledges that I understand the information contained in this handbook and agree to comply by it.

I understand this handbook isn't intended to cover each and every situation I may encounter as a volunteer, but is intended to be guide.

Signature _____

Date: _____

Program Evaluation Form

We're always looking for ways to improve our orientation program. Your filling out this evaluation helps us find ways to make the experience even better in the future.

Did the orientation program meet your expectations? Why or why not?

_____

_____

_____

Was the orientation program complete?

_____

_____

What information did you find most helpful?

_____

_____

What information did you feel was missing?

_____

_____

What questions do you have that weren't answered?

_____

_____

What would you add to improve the orientation program?

_____

_____

What would you remove to improve the orientation program?

_____

_____

Training Session Evaluation

Please help today's Trainer to improve future training sessions by answering the following questions about today's session.

Date: _____ Session Topic: _____

Name of Trainer: _____ Your name: _____

How long have you been a volunteer at [Name of your church]? _____

1. What was the main objective of this session?

_____
_____
_____
_____

2. What were other objectives you remember?

_____
_____
_____

3. How would you rate the pace of today's session?
Too slow   Slow   About right   Fast   Too fast
Why was that?

_____
_____
_____

4. How challenging did you find today's session?
Not at all   Not very   Neutral   Somewhat   Very
Why was that?

_____
_____
_____
_____

5. How relevant was the training to needs you're feeling now?

Not at all   Not very   Neutral   Somewhat   Very

How could the training have been more relevant to your needs?

_____

_____

_____

6. In your estimation, how well prepared was the Trainer?

Not at all   Not very   Neutral   Somewhat   Very

Why was that?

_____

_____

_____

7. Please write below about any part of the session about which you're still unclear, or have questions:

_____

_____

_____

8. Please offer any suggestions or further comments regarding this session:

_____

_____

_____

9. What other issues or items would you like to address on another day?

_____

_____

_____

Volunteer Continuing Education Sheet

Name of volunteer: _____

Volunteer positions held: Dates:

_____   _____

_____   _____

_____   _____

_____   _____

Church training sessions attended: Date: _____

_____   _____

_____   _____

_____   _____

_____   _____

External training attended (describe): Date:

_____   _____

_____   _____

_____   _____

_____   _____

Best Ever Evaluation Sheet

You're the best—and we want to know how you got that way!

In an effort to provide the best training sessions possible, we like to find out what training is most helpful and has had the greatest impact on your effectiveness.

Please take a few minutes and consider the list of training sessions you've attended. If you can't remember what was covered at each session, consult the Training Session Catalog. Then answer the following questions as honestly as you can.

Return this sheet to _____ as soon as possible.

Thank you.

1. Which training session was most memorable for you?
_____
Why?
_____
_____
_____
_____

2. Which training session was most relevant to you?
_____
Why?
_____
_____
_____
_____

3. Which training session provided information or skills you've used most often?
_____
What is that information, or those skills?
_____
_____
_____

4. Which training session would you recommend to someone else entering our area of ministry?

Why?

5. Which training session seemed least helpful to you?

Why?

Sample Interactive Routing Slip
Notice how there's accountability built in to this routing slip—and a chance to write a review.

Volunteer Ministry Routing Slip
The attached published piece is making the rounds . . . but not if you slow it down! Please read the attached and add your comments within one week. Then slip it into the Volunteer Office mail slot of the next person on the list.

Thank you!

Mary Jones
Volunteer Director
Date: _____

To:	Date received:	Date passed along:
Jackie Sampson		
Aaron Loop		
Jeff Knowles		
Jim Wood		
Jodi Forbes		
Shanell Frahm		
Brian Shiazi		
Janelle Spencer		

Share your comments below. Write your initials after your comments, please.

A WOW! Idea I found:

Sample
Volunteer Guidelines

Sample Volunteer Orientation Guidelines

First Christian Church Volunteer Orientation
Nursery Guidelines

What a blessing you'll be to parents as you provide a caring, nurturing, Christ-centered experience for their infants as parents worship. And you'll help babies associate feeling safe and secure with being at church.

Our first concern is safety. The following policies will help us make our nursery safe for babies and nursery workers alike.

- Nursery staff responsible for working an assigned shift must provide staffing or find a replacement from the list of approved substitutes. If a husband and wife are scheduled to work together and neither can come, then they must find two replacements. Notify the nursery director of any staffing changes.

- Three adults will work in the nursery on Sunday mornings (a nursery supervisor, an infant staffer, and a toddler staffer). On Wednesday night two adults will work in the nursery (a nursery supervisor and one infant staffer). This ratio must be maintained—no exceptions.

- Youth volunteers will be limited to one at any given time.

- Only the posted number of babies and toddlers can be in the nursery at any one time. If more children are presented, do not admit them until a certified nursery staff member has joined the existing staff to maintain the posted ratio of children/staff. Never exceed the posted ratio.

- Nursery staff must arrive 20 minutes before the Sunday service, Wednesday night program, or special service. On Sundays arrive at 9:10 A.M., and on Wednesdays arrive at 6:25 P.M.

- All nursery staff will wear nametags and greet each parent and child warmly.

- On a child's first visit to the nursery the parent must fill out a Nursery Information Sheet, which will then be kept on file in the nursery cabinet for future reference.

- Give parents a copy of the Nursery Handbook when they check their child in for the first time.

- Give parents a copy of the Nursery Handbook when they check their child in for the first time.

- No male volunteers are allowed to change babies' diapers.

- Parents will sign three adhesive tags when they check in children. Give one tag to the parent, affix one to the child's back, and put the third tag on the child's diaper bag.

- Parents of infants will complete the Infant Information Sheet when they check babies into the nursery.

- Use the digital pager system to notify parents to return to the nursery if necessary. Nursery supervisors have all been trained how to use it, and instructions are posted by the pager console. Nursery supervisors have the authority to decide when parents need to be notified.

- If a child is hurt but not seriously enough to page the parent, a parental notification form will be completed by the nursery supervisor on duty and given to the parent. A copy of the document will be kept in the church office.

- Diaper changing procedures are posted.

- The sickness policy is posted at the nursery door where both staff and parents can easily see it. Enforce the policy—no exceptions. If a child is turned away from the nursery, give the parent a copy of the policy.

- Fire and tornado procedures are posted, and two drills will be held annually.

- All nursery staff must complete the required safety background checks (which include a police check) and the three-hour First Christian Church Certification Program.

- Pictures of the nursery staff and their certification information will be posted to reassure parents of our preparation and professionalism.

- Children will remain inside the nursery until retrieved by an authorized person. Parents must have their retrieval tag, which must match the child's back tag. Parents must sign out their child.

- At the end of each nursery session, the nursery supervisor will complete a nursery supply summary and leave it in the church office. Nursery staff will also put clean bedding on any cribs that have been used. Deal with used bedding as instructed on the posted laundry instruction sheet.

- At the end of each nursery session, toys will be cleaned with a diluted bleach solution of 10-1 water/bleach ratio.

Volunteer Bill of Rights

I have the right to . . .

- Have my volunteer experience in the church encourage a healthy relationship with Jesus Christ.

- Use my God-given abilities, skills, and passions in significant ministry that gives something to the corporate body of Christ.

- Be respected as a full partner in ministry.

- Be young. Be old. Be any age and still valued in ministry.

- Be placed in a ministry role based on my gifts and abilities, not my church's need to find warm bodies to fill a slot in the organizational chart.

- Have a job description that provides me with the information I need to know whether I'm doing what's most important for me to be doing.

- Be provided with the resources and training I need to be successful.

- Receive regular evaluations so I can know how I'm doing and where I can improve.

- Serve in an environment where I'm well aware of the safety risks.

- Be respected if I say "no" to a request to serve in a specific volunteer role.

- Be valued—as a child of God and part of the body of Christ.

- Be expected to set boundaries that allow me a healthy work/life balance.

- Be retained as a volunteer not by guilt, but by the joy of serving others, serving God, and serving the church.